W9-BGK-835

Presence & Power

Presence & Power

Releasing the Holy Spirit in Your Life and Church

HAROLD E. BAUMAN

HERALD PRESS
Scottdale, Pennsylvania
Kitchener, Ontario

Library of Congress Cataloging-in-Publication Data

Bauman, Harold E. (Harold Ernest), 1922-
Presence and power.

1. Holy Spirit. 2. Gifts, Spiritual. 3. Fruit of the Spirit. 4. Pentecostalism. 5. Christian life—Mennonite authors. I. Title.
BT121.2.B38 1989 234'.12 88-34747
ISBN 0-8361-3493-1

The paper used in this publication meets the minimum requirements of American National Standard for Information Sciences—Permanence of Paper for Printed Library Materials, ANSI Z39.48-1984.

Unless otherwise indicated, Scripture quotations are from the Revised Standard Version of the Bible, copyrighted 1946, 1952, © 1971, 1973.

Scripture quotations marked "NIV" are from the *Holy Bible: New International Version*. Copyright © 1973, 1978, 1984 by the International Bible Society. Used by permission of Zondervan Bible Publishers.

Scripture quotations marked "Jerusalem Bible" are from *The Jerusalem Bible*, copyright © 1966 by Darton, Longman & Todd, Ltd. and Doubleday & Company, Inc. Used by permission of the publisher.

PRESENCE AND POWER
Copyright © 1989 by Herald Press, Scottdale, Pa. 15683
Published simultaneously in Canada by Herald Press, Kitchener, Ont. N2G 4M5. All rights reserved.
Library of Congress Catalog Card Number: 88-34747
International Standard Book Number: 0-8361-3493-1
Printed in the United States of America
Design by Paula M. Johnson

1 2 3 4 5 6 7 8 9 10 96 95 94 93 92 91 90 89

To my parents,
Norman G. and Ella Shoup Bauman,
whose lives portrayed the Spirit of Christ
in placing the kingdom first
and witnessing in their "Jerusalem and Samaria"
while they waited for the never-to-be-opened door
to follow their sense of call "to the ends of the earth"

Contents

Foreword 11
Preface 13

Introduction 17
Some Observations 18
Our Questions 20

1. Introducing the Holy Spirit 23
Some Affirmations Regarding the Holy Spirit . 23
How Are We to Relate Teachings
and Experience? 25
A Central Question 26

2. The Variety of Experiences in the New Testament 29
Variety in Experiences 30
Which Pattern of Experience? 38
Evidences of the Spirit 42
Conditions for Receiving the Spirit 43

**3. God's Plan for Us to Receive the Baptism
With the Spirit** 45
The Promise of the Spirit 45

Salvation Meets the Needs 46
The Basic Elements in Salvation 49
God's Plan for Us to Receive the Baptism . . . 56
The Spirit as the Central Gift 59
Faith Dramas Witnessing to Salvation 61

4. The Variety of Experiences Today 63
Reasons for a Variety of Experiences 63
Two Questions 73
The Fullness of the Spirit 74
Summary of Views 76
Accepting Differing Experiences 79

5. The Fruit and Gifts of the Spirit 85
The Spirit Gives Love 86
The Fruit of Love in Our Lives 87
Congregational Relationships and Evangelism . 90
The Spirit Gives Spiritual Gifts 92
Spiritual Gifts and the Priesthood
of All Believers 100

6. Understanding the Holy Spirit Renewal Movement 103
Historical Context 104
The Charismatic Movement 108
Elements in Renewal 114
Claiming the Promise 116

Scripture Index 119
The Author 123

On the last and greatest day of the Feast, Jesus stood and said in a loud voice, "If anyone is thirsty, let him come to me and drink. Whoever believes in me, as the Scripture has said, streams of living water will flow from within him." By this he meant the Spirit whom those who believed in him were later to receive. Up to that time the Spirit had not been given, since Jesus had not yet been glorified.

—*John 7:37-39, NIV*

You will receive power when the Holy Spirit comes on you; and you will be my witnesses in Jerusalem, and in all Judea and Samaria, and to the ends of the earth.

—*Acts 1:8, NIV*

And in him [Christ] you too are being built together to become a dwelling in which God lives by his Spirit.

—*Ephesians 2:22, NIV*

Foreword

Harold Bauman has taken a keen interest in the charismatic renewal among Mennonites from its beginnings in the early 1970s. As a part of his responsibility as secretary of the Mennonite Board of Congregational Ministries he has attended many of the Holy Spirit conferences and meetings since then. He has functioned as mediator between the church at large and Mennonite Renewal Service, an infomal group organized to promote charismatic emphases and expressions. He has participated in the dialogue and debate centering around charismatic issues. He has been a master teacher and an able expositor and interpreter of the Bible.

Presence and Power is a distillation of his thinking on the subject with particular reference to a believers church perspective. It has been his conviction that a truly biblical understanding of the Holy Spirit is primary and will illuminate, interpret, and correct experience; that doctrine and practice should be grounded on careful exegesis of the Bible rather than on experience.

Pastors and laity, radical charismatics, pseudocharismatics, and anticharismatics will all find challenge and insight on these pages.

Bauman concludes that salvation involves four basic steps: (1) repentance: confessing Jesus as Lord, (2) baptism for forgiveness: Jesus as Savior, (3) receiving the Spirit: Jesus as Baptizer, and (4) identifying with God's people: Jesus as Head. Each of these steps involves an informed decision by faith, a progressive course of action based upon knowledge.

This will be a valuable book for pastors and church leaders. It should be placed in church libraries and used as a source book for adult Sunday school classes and home Bible study groups.

—Daniel Yutzy

Preface

It has been my privilege during the past fifteen years not only to grow in the work of the Spirit in my own journey, but also to converse with many other people in their journey with the Spirit.

These settings have included workshops for pastors and elders and their spouses, weekend retreats, and renewal conferences and festivals. I have been enriched by all of these. They have allowed me to develop further and test over and over the teachings that have emerged from these experiences. I am grateful to the many persons who have contributed to my faith and life.

Over the years I have read many books on the Holy Spirit. Most of them present varied views which fall generally into the Pentecostal view, the Fundamentalist-Evangelical view, or the Lutheran or Catholic charismatic views. I am writing to present a believers church perspective on experiencing the Holy Spirit and some implications for church life and discipleship.

I have tried to write a readable book for pastors, elders, Sunday school teachers, parents, youth, and all others who have not yet been named. For this reason I have not used footnotes. I have named only one author and book—and that because the issue being addressed at that point is a heavy one.

I am grateful to the persons who critiqued the manuscript and made good suggestions for improvement. The reviewers represented a variety of viewpoints, so the views in the book do not always agree with theirs. I take final responsibility for the views presented.

I express my gratitude to the Mennonite Board of Congregational Ministries and Mennonite Board of Missions for making possible the participation in the ministry events and the time for writing.

As this book goes forth, I pray that what is helpful the Spirit will use to connect many persons with the blessings available. What is not helpful may the Spirit providentially overrule. I will be glad to dialogue with readers about the content as well as their experiences.

—Harold E. Bauman
Box 370
Elkhart, IN 46515

Presence POWER

Introduction

Imagine that you and I are sitting on some stones in the shade near Jacob's Well in Samaria twenty centuries ago. As we rest, a Roman officer and several soldiers ride up to the well and get off their horses. The officer, whose name is Cornelius, enters into a conversation with a local man by the name of Manasses who also came for a drink of water.

"You look like a stranger in these parts," said Manasses.

"Yes, I am Cornelius from Caesarea," responded Cornelius. "I get up to Jerusalem now and then on business and to see what is going on."

The eyes of Manasses lit up. "I am Manasses. Jerusalem is all right, but our city in Samaria can have some excitement too. We surely did several years ago!"

"Tell me about it." Cornelius was curious.

"A man named Philip came from Jerusalem and preached about Jesus of Nazareth. People were healed, sins were forgiven, and there was great joy." The face of Manasses was alive!

Cornelius appeared cautious. "I've heard of this Jesus. Do you know him?"

"Know him!" exclaimed Manasses. "I'll say I do. Some weeks later several of the leading apostles—Peter and John—came to see what was going on. They laid their hands on us and we received the Holy Spirit. I experienced deep inner peace and joy and the presence and power of God within me like an artesian well."

"Don't I know it! I received the Holy Spirit and I know this Jesus, too!" exclaimed Cornelius.

"You do? A Gentile Roman soldier? Praise the Lord! So you became a follower of Jesus and then later received the Holy Spirit."

Manasses was ecstatic.

Cornelius looked perplexed. "I received the baptism with the Spirit when I received the good news that Jesus is Lord, not later."

Manasses looked puzzled, yet determined. "I am not sure I can believe that is possible. It is not the way it happened to us. Ours must be the right way because Peter and John were here."

"Well," responded Cornelius, "Peter was with me, too. He told us all about Jesus and before he finished the Holy Spirit came upon all of us. Even the Jews with Peter could not think of any reason why we shouldn't be baptized."

Manasses shook his head as he walked away. "I don't know what to make of it. You sound like you know the Spirit. But first one becomes a Christian and then later has the second experience of the baptism with the Spirit."

Cornelius was aghast. "Why does Manasses think we all have to be like he is? My experience was as valid as his. We both serve Christ as Lord and we both claim by faith that the Holy Spirit lives within us. We both know the presence and power of the Spirit to live as disciples and to do ministry."

Some Observations

Let me share several observations. The first observation is that we tend to form our beliefs from our own experiences. The story of Cornelius and Manasses reminds all of us how much we form our beliefs from our experiences. I may do some of this in this book, though the basic pattern of my experience is different from what I will present here. Later I will give some reasons why people have differing experiences with the Holy Spirit.

A second observation is that people tend to borrow the beliefs taught by the group in which they come alive in the Spirit. This should not surprise us. We may be disappointed if the group is different from our own. Or, we can instead affirm the new joy and vitality of renewed persons and delay for some months the discussion of how to understand their experience theologically. The church is the community of the Spirit to bring re-creation. We should not drive people away because we cannot agree on when and how it should happen. Loving conversations some months after the freshness of the experience can help toward mutual understanding and mutual beliefs.

I believe it is possible to receive all that God has for us and to do this within the faith of the believers church. We believe this faith is in line with the Scriptures. We do need to learn from others. We also need to test their beliefs while we learn from them. I do not believe we need to borrow other theologies in order to receive all that God has to give us in relation to the Holy Spirit. It is important, however, that we build our beliefs with care. The reader who stays with me throughout the book will discover one way to view what God offers in the Holy Spirit.

A third observation is that whenever there is a recovery of a neglected area of Christian faith and experience, there will be some excesses. Some people say they want nothing to do with the renewal movement because it is "disorderly," "rejects medical science," "focuses only on the emotions," and "replaces the Bible with personal visions." One can find these and other extremes in some renewal groups and some individuals.

How shall we view the renewal movement in light of these excesses? Those persons who are heirs of the spiritual witness of the Radical Reformation of the sixteenth century should know better than to turn off a renewal movement because of excesses. The excesses of the Radical Reformation played a part in causing the Protestant Reformers to reject the witness of the Anabaptist movement. Only within the last 75 years have many scholars recognized legitimate elements among that diverse movement called Anabaptism. We say the response of the Reformers was not fair.

We have the opportunity and responsibility today to be open to the witness of the Holy Spirit with regard to the central realities of the Holy Spirit renewal movement. What a tragedy if we allow some excesses to close us to the present movement of the Holy Spirit in many countries throughout the world! The Spirit desires to move among us also.

There are members of many religious communions who are experiencing new life in the Spirit. Where church attendance was a bore, now fellowship with God's people is a joy. Where the Bible was a closed book, now the Scriptures come alive with meaning. Where prayers seemed to bounce back from the ceiling, now prayer is deeply meaningful. Where persons were afraid to be identified as Christians, there is now boldness to witness about Christ as the life-changer.

Our Questions

The questions we each face are: Do I know the reality of the Holy Spirit in my life? Do I know the Spirit as joy and peace and justice in my daily life? Do I know the Spirit as power for living and witness and ministry? Am I experiencing the release of spiritual gifts in my life as opportunities for caring ministry come to me day by day?

These questions are much more important than the question, How many experiences have I had?

In exploring the Holy Spirit as God's central gift in becoming a Christian, we will look briefly at who the Holy Spirit is. Then we will examine the variety of experiences with the Spirit in the Gospels and Acts. In light of these experiences we will then study the teachings of the New Testament on the Spirit in Christian experience. Following this we will explore why there is a variety of experiences today in receiving the Spirit in what is called "the baptism with the Holy Spirit." There will then follow a study of the fruit of the Spirit and the gifts of the Spirit, the relation of each to the other, and their function in the believing community. In conclusion we will look at a brief survey of the larger historical setting of the current movements which may help clarify our perspectives. A brief listing of some elements in renewal may give us guidance as we end the study.

CHAPTER 1

Introducing the Holy Spirit

Who is the Holy Spirit? What does the Holy Spirit do? In order to have some understandings as a place to begin and to show the basic beliefs from which I write, I want to present some affirmations about the Holy Spirit. We will need to test these as we move through the study.

Some Affirmations Regarding the Holy Spirit

The creation account in Genesis begins with the Spirit of God moving over the face of the waters (Gen. 1:2). The prophet Ezekiel writes that the Spirit of the Lord fell upon him (Ezek. 11:5). Jesus says that fathers who are basically evil (selfish) will respond positively to the requests of their children for food. How much more, says Jesus, will God give all good things (the Holy Spirit) to those who keep on asking (verb tense, Matt. 7:11; Luke 11:13).

In writing of the life in the Spirit, Paul can move freely from "the Spirit of God" to the "Spirit of Christ" (Rom. 8:9). Even more directly, Paul writes to the Corinthians that "the Lord is the Spirit, and where the Spirit of the Lord is, there is freedom" (2 Cor. 3:17, NIV).

Thus I affirm that the Holy Spirit is the Spirit of God, and the Spirit of Christ. The biblical writers view the Holy Spirit as personality as much as God is a personality. Jesus and Paul are not concerned about drawing sharp distinctions between "Christ in you" and the "Holy Spirit in you" (John 14:17-20; Gal. 2:20; 4:6).

A second affirmation is that it is only by the work of the Holy Spirit that one can become a Christian. Paul writes to the Corinthians, "I want you to understand that no one speaking by the Spirit of God ever says 'Jesus be cursed!' and no one can say 'Jesus is Lord' except by the Holy Spirit" (1 Cor. 12:3, NIV). The Holy Spirit woos and draws us to Christ. The decision to accept Christ as Lord and Savior and Baptizer of one's life is a spiritual struggle in which the Holy Spirit gently enables us.

The hymn writer says:

> I sought the Lord, and afterward I knew
> He moved my soul to seek him, seeking me;
> It was not I that found, O Savior true,
> No, I was found of thee.

The Spirit not only draws us to Christ but also does the inner renewal (Titus 3:5). It is the Spirit who brings the new birth (John 3:5).

If I am a believer in Christ, is the Holy Spirit in my life? A third affirmation is that the Holy Spirit is present in every Christian. Paul writes in Romans 8:9, "But you are not in the flesh, you are in the Spirit, if in fact the Spirit of God dwells in you. Any one who does not have the Spirit of Christ does not belong to him."

According to Paul, there is no difference between "having the Spirit" and the Spirit being "in you." The Spirit dwells in the believer as a result of the new birth. However, whether one has laid hold of the presence and power of the Spirit in one's life is another matter. I will return to this later in the study.

A fourth affirmation is that the Holy Spirit was active in the Old Testament and was with the disciples before Pentecost. The difference in the presence of the Spirit before and after Pentecost was not "none of the Spirit in the Old Testament" and then "all of the Spirit in the New Testament." Rather, the difference has to do with the difference between the old and new covenants, and the nature and scope of the Spirit's work made possible by the life, death, and resurrection of Jesus.

In summary, I have affirmed that the Holy Spirit has personality and may also be spoken of as the Spirit of God and the Spirit of Christ. I have affirmed that one becomes a believer by the work of the Holy Spirit and that the Holy Spirit is present in every Christian. Whether one knows the Spirit as God's presence and power in one's life is a different question. Finally, I have affirmed that the Holy Spirit was active in the old covenant and that the difference seen in the new covenant has to do with the nature and scope of the Spirit's work as the result of Christ's ministry in bringing salvation.

How Are We to Relate Teachings and Experience?

In doing the study which follows we will begin with one kind of material in the New Testament on the Spirit—the story or "narrative" material—in which persons and groups received water baptism. Some received the Holy Spirit at that time while others did not. This material is in the Gospels and the book of Acts.

Following this, we will look at the "teaching" material in the prophets, Gospels, Acts, and the epistles to the churches. Jesus taught the disciples about the Spirit. They then experienced the Spirit, following which their understandings were further illuminated. This suggests that the narrative materials are instructive as they are correlated with the teaching materials.

Thus, two principles will guide in understanding the Bible. First, we will use no one isolated experience or teaching to establish a basic statement of faith. Rather, we will take into account the broader teachings and faith understandings.

Second, the teachings about the Spirit in the prophets, Gospels, Acts, and epistles will be normative in arriving at understandings. However, the work of the Spirit in the lives of people will help illuminate the teachings.

For example, in the Jerusalem conference described in Acts 15, the reports of the work of the grace of God among the Gentiles (experience) made an impact on the interpretation of the Scriptures. Only then were new understandings accepted by most of the people present in the conference.

Thus the teachings and the stories inform each other. They must be correlated as much as possible to arrive at normative teaching and to reduce apparent conflict. We need to be open to the possibility that our traditional interpretations of a given passage may block us from receiving some new insight the Spirit may want to give us. Even then, the Spirit moves in sovereign ways, and our faith formulations do not always explain everything.

A Central Question

One of the twentieth-century controversies revolves around how to define what the Scriptures call "the baptism with the Holy Spirit." Since there are several definitions, it is difficult to write without confusion. One would like to avoid using the phrase at all, but that does not seem possible. John the Baptist did say of our Savior, "He will baptize you with the Holy Spirit." Therefore, we cannot escape the issue nor can we avoid using some phrase to designate it.

I invite the reader to walk through the study of the Scriptures with me and to allow the understandings to emerge. Test my interpretation of the Scriptures as we move along.

In due time, we will face the issue, "What is the baptism with the Spirit?" My goal is to arrive at some understandings that can be affirmed together regarding the Holy Spirit in Christian experience and congregational life. We may be able to do this even if there are differences on the technical use of the phrase, *the baptism with the Spirit.*

We will begin by noting the variety of experiences in the New Testament in relation to receiving the Holy Spirit.

CHAPTER 2

The Variety of Experiences in the New Testament

Once while I was serving as a minister on a college campus, a student asked me, "What do you believe as to when one receives the baptism with the Holy Spirit?" Before I could answer, he turned to Acts 8:14–17, read it, and said, "The Samaritans received the baptism with the Holy Spirit after their conversion. That is the way it always is. I know because that was my experience."

I responded that I was glad he knew the personal reality of the Holy Spirit. I invited him to read Acts 10:30–48. We noted that Cornelius received the gift of the Holy Spirit when he heard the gospel. When Cornelius received Jesus he also received the baptism with the Holy Spirit. The student blinked his eyes and said, "I never saw that before."

My conversation with the student focuses some questions many people have today. Why is there a variety of experiences in the New Testament in receiving the Holy Spirit? How do they relate to our experiences today? Is it God's intention that we are first to become a Christian and then at some later time receive the baptism with the Spirit as a second major experience? Historically, this has been called a two-stage theology of Christian experience. In this view the baptism with the Spirit comes sometime after conversion. Or is it God's intention that we are to receive Christ as Lord and Savior and the baptism with the Spirit as part of our conversion experience as Cornelius did? Or still a third option, Is the baptism with the Spirit the receiving of Christ as Lord and Savior in which the Spirit effects the new birth and is in the believer's life? Are there still other options?

Let us note the similarities and differences in the experiences of people who received water baptism "into" the name of a person in the New Testament. We can then see whether that person received the Holy Spirit and what signs, if any, were present with the experience. We will use the phrase, "the baptism with the Spirit," to describe the experience of those receiving the Spirit at Pentecost and afterward. We will seek to understand its meaning more fully at a later time.

Variety in Experiences

Disciples of John the Baptist. We will begin with the persons who became disciples of John the Baptist (Matt. 3:6 and 11). The baptism of John was a *preparation* for the coming king. He preached a baptism of repentance for the forgiveness of sins. There is no mention of these persons receiving the Holy Spirit. John said the one coming would baptize with the Holy Spirit and with fire, thus making the baptism with the Spirit in the future.

The baptism of John was a preparation. It looked ahead to what was to come. The sign accompanying the baptism was a turning away from sin. Changed behavior proved repentance had taken place.

Jesus. At the baptism of Jesus (Matt. 3:13–17), there is no indication of a name into which he was baptized. Had he followed John, Jesus would likely have been called a disciple of John. Clearly this did not happen.

Jesus said the purpose of his baptism was "to fulfill all righteousness." In his baptism which he voluntarily requested, Jesus identified with us as one who publicly confessed his delight in allegiance to God and God's kingdom (Isa. 11:3). In his baptism, there was a witness to Jesus as the Old Testament deliverer when the Holy Spirit came upon him (Isa. 42:1).

The voice from heaven identified Jesus as king. "This is my beloved son" is a quotation from Psalm 2:7 which was used in the crowning of the king. The last part of the statement, "in whom I am well pleased," from Isaiah 42:1, clarifies what kind of king Jesus was. Jesus was a servant king, living by the power of the Holy Spirit who was promised as part of the covenant.

Thus for Jesus the new covenant began at his baptism in which the Holy Spirit came upon him as the power by which he lived and served. Jesus began calling disciples to form the new people of God who would also receive the Spirit after he was glorified. Thus Jesus was the unique bearer of the Holy Spirit during the three years of his ministry.

In summary, Jesus was baptized to witness to his allegiance to God and to receive the gift of the Holy Spirit for power for his servant ministry. The signs that he had received the Spirit included the coming of the Spirit like a dove, the voice from heaven, the temptations in the wilderness, his deeds of service, his teaching with authority, and his delight in his faith relationship with God. Except for the first two, several or more of these signs can be present in our lives to witness to the presence of the Holy Spirit.

Disciples of Jesus. Jesus called people to follow him and apparently baptized the first of them. He then gave the disciples the responsibility to baptize (John 3:22; 4:1–2). They became known as disciples of Jesus. The purpose was to become followers of Jesus. Discipleship involved identifying with Jesus: adopting his life-style and following his teachings. There is no mention of the Holy Spirit coming upon the disciples before the resurrection of Jesus. In fact, John explicitly writes that the Spirit had not been given, since Jesus had not yet been glorified (John 7:37–39).

For John, the crucifixion and the resurrection of Jesus were the glorification of Jesus. Jesus was "lifted up" (John 12:27–33). In the upper room Jesus told his disciples that he could send the Holy Spirit only if he went away (John 16:7). Thus it is not surprising that after the resurrection John reports that Jesus met his disciples and said, "As the Father has sent me, even so I send you." He then breathed on them and said, "Receive the Holy Spirit" (John 20:21–23).

While receiving the Holy Spirit brings life, here the Spirit is clearly given as empowerment for the ministry of evangelism. Thus those who receive the Spirit can be assured that God has forgiven their sins and unbelievers that their sins remain. John has written his book as a complete whole. God sends Jesus who receives the Spirit for ministry (John 1:32–34; 3:34). Jesus sends the disciples who receive the Spirit for ministry (John 20:21–23). The Spirit who was not yet given (John 7:39) is now given. Thus John's book has a "Pentecost" and a "great commission."

The 120. This leads us to Luke's report of the coming of the Holy Spirit on Pentecost. The one hundred and twenty were in the upper room, waiting for the gift Jesus had promised. Jesus said, "In a few days you will be baptized with the Holy Spirit. . . . You will receive power when the Holy Spirit comes on you and you will be my witnesses . . ." (Acts 1:4–5, 8, NIV).

Likely all of them had been followers of Jesus for some

time. On the day of Pentecost the Holy Spirit came upon them. They were filled with the Holy Spirit and they spoke in tongues, telling the mighty works of God. They witnessed with power.

In summary, these persons were disciples of Jesus. They received the Spirit sometime after their first identification with Jesus in their baptism. The signs were speaking in tongues, declaring the wonders of God, and witnessing with power. They had received the baptism with the Spirit Jesus had promised.

The 3000. In his sermon Peter explained the coming of the Holy Spirit (Acts 2:14–36). His hearers, composed of God-fearing Jews and converts to Judaism, responded, "What shall we do?" Peter's invitation (Acts 2:38–41) to come to Christ was fourfold:

First, repent. Change your mind. Turn in the opposite direction. Instead of crucifying Jesus as your elders did, confess that he is Lord. Second, be baptized in the name of Jesus Christ for the forgiveness of your sins. Third, you shall receive the gift of the Holy Spirit. Fourth, identify with God's new people.

In summary, the three thousand were invited to a whole salvation. They were to confess that Jesus is Lord, experience forgiveness of sins, receive the gift of the Holy Spirit, and identify with God's new people. There is no record that they spoke in tongues, though some or all may have.

The evidences of a Spirit-filled congregation according to Luke (Acts 2:42–47) are:

- A love for the study of the Scriptures
- Enjoying fellowship together
- The presence of miracles
- An unselfish sharing as people have needs
- Gathering for corporate worship and prayers
- Gathering in small groups in homes to break bread

with joy
- People being saved as the result of Christian fellowship and witness

So the three thousand entered the new covenant. They experienced Christ as Lord, as Savior, as Baptizer with the Holy Spirit, and as head of the church through identifying with the gathering of the 120.

The Samaritans. Quite in contrast to the experience of the three thousand is the experience of the Samaritans (Acts 8:5–17). The Holy Spirit moved Philip to go to a city in Samaria to proclaim Christ. Many experienced healing, evil spirits were cast out, and there was great joy in the city. Many received baptism as the result of Philip preaching the kingdom of God and the name of Jesus Christ.

When the apostles in Jerusalem heard that Samaria had received the Word of God, they sent them Peter and John. When they arrived, they prayed for the Samaritans that they might receive the Holy Spirit. The Spirit had not yet come upon any of them; they had simply been baptized into the name of the Lord Jesus. Then they laid their hands on them and they received the Holy Spirit.

We note here that they had been baptized into Jesus and had become followers of Christ. We also note that they received the baptism with the Spirit sometime following their conversion. There is no mention that they spoke in tongues, though they may have. There apparently was some evidence of the Spirit coming into people's lives, however. For Simon saw that the Spirit was given through the laying on of hands and offered the apostles money. However, we are not told what the signs were.

The Samaritans were a mixed race. They were half Jew and half Gentile. Thus God confirmed the incorporation of the Samaritans into the church by clearly giving the Holy Spirit to them, in the presence of two apostles. This was the Samaritan Pentecost. (We will treat this more fully later.) The Spirit led Peter and John to preach in many Samaritan villages as they returned to Jerusalem.

Paul. What kind of experience did the apostle Paul have (Acts 9:1–22; 22:6–16)? Was he first converted on the road to Damascus and did he then receive the Spirit three days later? Or was it all part of the total conversion experience?

Paul was struck down by a bright light. He heard the question, "Why do you persecute me?" Paul responded, "Who are you, Lord?" The word *Lord* was addressed to Jesus often in the Gospels, meaning "master" or "teacher" or "sir." It is not likely Paul was making a confession of faith on the Damascus road.

Paul was told he was persecuting Jesus, that he should go to the city where he would receive further word. For three days he was without sight and did not eat or drink. On the third day Ananias came to him so he could regain his sight and be filled with the Spirit. Immediately Paul regained his sight and was baptized for the forgiveness of his sins (Acts 22:16).

The New Testament often views conversion as passing from darkness to light. The believer moved from the community of darkness to the community of light. Something like scales fell from Paul's eyes right before his baptism. He was promised that he would also be filled with the Holy Spirit. Thus Paul experienced the basic elements in a conversion experience on the third day.

The sign given by Luke that Paul had received the Spirit was that he immediately proclaimed Jesus as the Son of God, witnessing with power. He showed that Jesus of Nazareth was the Messiah. At this point there is no mention of tongues. We need to keep in mind that Paul wrote to the Corinthians that he spoke in tongues more than all of them, but he does not say when he received that gift.

Let us summarize what we have found thus far. The one hundred and twenty received the Spirit sometime after they became disciples of Jesus. The three thousand were invited to become believers and to receive the Holy Spirit at the same time. The Samaritans became believers and then received the Spirit as a second experience later on. Paul received baptism, the forgiveness of sins, and was filled with the Holy Spirit in one experience on the third day. The coming of the Spirit into the lives of these people was accompanied by various evidences of the Spirit's power.

Cornelius. Cornelius was a Gentile, an officer in the Roman army. On the basis of Luke's description, Cornelius was a devout believer in God (with old covenant knowledge). Yet he was searching for something more (Acts 10:1–48).

Peter's message to Cornelius and his household was a simple recounting of God's good news in Jesus. He told how Jesus went about doing good and healing. He talked about his death and resurrection, and the forgiveness of sins for those who believe in his name. While Peter was preaching, the Holy Spirit fell on all who heard the Word. All the Jewish believers were amazed that the Gentiles had received the Spirit. Peter asked if anyone had any reason why they should not be baptized. They then received baptism in the name of Jesus Christ.

Cornelius and his household experienced conversion and the baptism with the Holy Spirit at the same time. They recognized Jesus as Lord and experienced the Holy Spirit. This is part of what it means to be saved according to Peter (Acts 11:14–18). It is to receive the Spirit as a gift and as power to use the gifts of the Spirit in ministry.

The signs given for their having received the Holy Spirit were speaking in tongues and praising God. No doubt this was similar to speaking in tongues on Pentecost in which they declared the mighty acts of God.

The Gentile Pentecost has now happened. The good

news of the kingdom and the gift of the Holy Spirit were now available to all—Jews *and* Gentiles.

The Twelve at Ephesus. Out of Paul's mission to the Gentiles there is one more experience of receiving the Holy Spirit to be noted (Acts 19:1–7). Paul came to Ephesus and found some disciples of John the Baptist. Apparently Paul noted something deficient in their lives. Some versions translate Paul's question, "Have ye received the Holy Ghost *since* ye believed?" (King James). This seems to imply a lapse of time following conversion. However, the word *since* can also mean "because you believed, did you receive the Holy Spirit?" Nearly all modern translations (including *The New King James Bible*) read, "Did you receive the Holy Spirit when you believed?" Paul's expectation was that people receive the Holy Spirit when they become believers.

These disciples responded, "No, we have never even heard that there is a Holy Spirit." Paul asked, "Into what then were you baptized?"

"Into John's baptism," they answered. Paul then interprets John's baptism as a baptism of *preparation* for the one to come, Jesus. They were then rebaptized in the name of Jesus and they received the Holy Spirit when Paul laid hands on them.

The signs of receiving the Holy Spirit on the part of the Ephesians were speaking in tongues and prophesying.

Paul viewed these disciples as believers who were anticipating the coming of Christ. They were still old-covenant believers, living 25 to 30 years behind "the times." Paul treats them as persons now becoming Christians—new-covenant believers—by rebaptizing them. Paul views their conversion and receiving of the Spirit as happening at the same time, as parts of a whole experience. Their rebaptism was their personal intentional response to the gospel. This passage is one basis for rebaptizing persons whose earlier baptism did not witness to a personal voluntary decision of faith in Christ and a personal covenant with God's people.

Which Pattern of Experience?

We can now observe that some persons became believers in Jesus and then received the Holy Spirit at a later time: the 120 and the Samaritans. We also observe that persons believed in Christ and received the Holy Spirit at the same time, as witnessed in their baptism: the 3000, Paul, Cornelius, and the disciples at Ephesus.

We can now ask, Which of these patterns is normative for us today? We remind ourselves we cannot decide solely on the basis of this story material. We must also consider the teaching materials, as we will in the next chapter. However, what does our study thus far say to us? Let us look at the two cases when persons received the Spirit as a second experience sometime after identifying with Jesus: the 120 and the Samaritans.

Can we use the 120 as our model of experience in conversion and receiving the Holy Spirit? They walked with Jesus and were closest to him. Surely the apostles should be our model in conversion and receiving the Holy Spirit!

We need to take seriously the reason John gives for the 120 receiving the baptism with the Holy Spirit after their decision to follow Jesus. John writes, "On the last day of the feast, the great day, Jesus stood up and proclaimed, 'If any one thirst, let him come to me and drink. He who believes in me, as the scripture has said, "Out of his heart shall flow rivers of living water." ' Now this he said about the Spirit, which those who believed in him were to receive; *for as yet the Spirit had not been given, because Jesus was not yet glorified*" (John 7:37–39; italics mine).

According to John, the baptism with the Spirit was not possible for the disciples of John the Baptist or the disciples of Jesus prior to Jesus receiving his resurrection body. They were living across the bridge between the old covenant and the new covenant—a unique period in God's covenant history. Their baptism was one of *anticipation,* a looking ahead to what the Messiah would provide in the new covenant. Our baptism is one of *fulfillment,* a looking back to what the Messiah has done in his finished work. Their baptism under John the Baptist was an old covenant baptism, even though we read of it in the New Testament. The baptism of the 3000, Paul, Cornelius, the disciples at Ephesus, and us is a new covenant baptism. It witnesses to all the elements in salvation. Receiving the baptism with the Spirit is included. Else why did Christ have to die and be raised?

If we heed John's statement (John 7:37–39), we conclude that the apostles are not our model for the relation of conversion and receiving the baptism with the Spirit. That is, the model that the baptism with the Spirit is received at a later time following conversion is not God's intention for us.

We still need to look at the Samaritans who became followers of Christ and then later received the baptism with the Holy Spirit (Acts 8:5–17). If in all the other experiences following the 120 the people received the baptism with the Spirit at the time of conversion (the 3000, Paul, Cornelius, and the disciples at Ephesus), why did the Samaritans not follow the same pattern?

One alternative is to say the "two-stage" conversion is normal. First, one is saved and then later one receives the baptism with the Spirit. In the light of the other four experiences in Acts and John's teaching (7:37–39), it is difficult, if not impossible, to support this view.

Another alternative held by some is to say the Samaritans were not really converted. They "believed Philip" (Acts 8:12), not Jesus Christ; one cannot become a Christian without receiving the Holy Spirit. When the apostles came they received the Spirit, so the Samaritans were not Christians before.

This view ignores the witness Luke gives. In verse 6, "the multitudes with one accord gave heed to what was said by Philip."

Instead of continuing their former practice of giving heed to Simon, they believed Philip when he preached good news about the kingdom of God and the name of Jesus Christ. They had received the word of God (vv. 9–14). They were baptized in the name of the Lord Jesus (vv. 12, 16). There was much joy in the city (v. 8). I find it hard to believe they were not Christians before Peter and John came.

A third view sees the problem in Philip. He had been ordained as a deacon with a specific task, yet he found himself functioning as an evangelist. The apostles knew he was untrained and unprepared for the work, so they came immediately to confirm and complete the work. Philip apparently had not taught them about the baptism with the Spirit.

Perhaps Philip did not teach the Samaritans about the baptism with the Spirit. We do know that being filled with the Spirit was one of the qualifications for those chosen to serve the Greek widows. Philip had experienced the baptism with the Spirit.

Then why did he not teach it? If he taught it, why did they not receive the baptism with the Holy Spirit? Luke tells us they were baptized only in the name of Jesus. Luke also tells us that the apostles in Jerusalem had heard that Samaria had received the word of God. This phrase, "word of God," in Acts refers to the full gospel message. Perhaps Philip's lack of training was the reason the apostles had to come to Samaria, but I believe this is doubtful. We have no record that the apostles followed up Philip's work with the Ethiopian eunuch. Tradition says that the eunuch established the Christian Church in Ethiopia.

However, this leads to a fourth way to understand why the Samaritans received the Holy Spirit some time after their conversion. This view sees God working out the spread of the gospel (Acts 1:8), overcoming major Jewish prejudices and Samaritan prejudices. The gospel came first to the Jews (Jerusalem and Judea), then to the Samaritans (half-Jews, Samaria), and then to the Gentiles (Cornelius, to whole world). How could the Jews accept the Samaritans whom they called "foolish"? The Samaritans could not accept the Jews or their way of worship. There was strong hatred between the two groups. The woman at the well said in effect to Jesus, "When the Messiah comes, he will show who is right." The schism between Jews and Samaritans was deep.

The apostles in Jerusalem were concerned about the word of God coming to Samaria. They sent Peter and John to witness what was going on. When they came, they prayed for them and they received the Holy Spirit.

Does Luke give us a clue when he writes that Philip preached the kingdom of God (God's rule) and the name of Jesus Christ (Christ's forgiveness)? The people were baptized only in the name of the Lord Jesus. They apparently were not taught or led to claim the promise of the Holy Spirit.

Was this by God's design? Did the Holy Spirit lead Philip not to minister the baptism with the Spirit? Did God plan for the Samaritans to receive the central gift of the new covenant, the Holy Spirit, in the presence of the apostles so they could be certified as true Christians (new covenant believers) without any doubt? We do need to note that Samaritans were certified without accepting the ceremonies of the Jews. The Gospels in presenting the ministry of Jesus did include his dealing with the Jew-Samaritan tension (as well as the Jew-Gentile tension). We would thus expect the initiation of the new covenant to resolve these tensions in a decisive way.

This leads to a basic observation. The key issue in Acts is not whether salvation is a whole experience or whether one is saved first and then later receives the baptism with the Spirit. The key issue is: now that the Messiah has effected the new covenant, who is eligible to enter God's movement and on what basis? Does one first need to become Jewish through ceremonies and then become eligible to receive the gospel? Or can one come out of any race and background and receive the gospel by faith, witnessed by the baptism with the Spirit, the central gift in the new covenant?

The certification of the Samaritans by faith happened when they received the Holy Spirit with Peter and John present. The certification of the Gentiles by faith happened when Cornelius received the Holy Spirit with Peter present. This opened the door for Paul's work among the Gentiles with Antioch as the base. Both Peter (Acts 11:1–18) and Paul (Acts 15) needed to explain what God did through them among the Gentiles and they were vindicated. The full salvation experience, including receiving the baptism with the Holy Spirit and acceptance into God's people, was available to all when they accepted the good news by faith.

Evidences of the Spirit

The evidences of having received the Holy Spirit varied. In the seven experiences (Jesus, the 120, the 3000, Samaritans, Paul, Cornelius, and the disciples at Ephesus), speaking in tongues is specifically mentioned three times. Four times it is not mentioned. With the Samaritans one might infer tongues speaking, though Simon may have been impressed with something else.

The approximately half-and-half ratio should appeal to tongues-speakers not to insist that all must speak in tongues, and to non-tongues-speakers to accept tongues as a valid gift that many persons will receive, even today.

Other evidences of the presence of the Spirit that we noted include: witness with power that Jesus is the Son of God; love of the Scriptures and prayer; love evident in the fellowship of believers (the fruit of the Spirit); joy in corporate worship and small groups in homes; readiness to share with those in need; the presence of miracles; and people coming to salvation. As we will note in the teaching materials, no one evidence seems to be the exclusive test of the presence of the Spirit, except the confession that Jesus is Lord. A close second is the fruit of the Spirit (love) in one's life (1 Cor. 12:3; 13:1–13).

Conditions for Receiving the Spirit

In concluding this study of experiences of receiving the Spirit in the New Testament, we will make the study more personal. What conditions were present for receiving full salvation, including the baptism with the Spirit, however we finally understand it?

First, in the words of Jesus, "If any one thirsts." In most cases, there was a desire to do God's will, to be in God's presence, to know God more fully, and to experience what God has to give. Let us ask ourselves, How much do I hunger and thirst for God's presence and power in my life? How much am I fully desiring God's will in my life above all else? Am I content with the status quo?

Second, there was teaching about what God had done through Jesus and about the promised gift of the Holy Spirit. Jesus was proclaimed as Lord and people were invited to respond. Let us ask ourselves, Have I faced Jesus not only as my Savior but also as my Lord? Am I informed on the Holy Spirit and what the Spirit offers to do in my life as a child of God?

Third, there was a faith response. People laid hold by faith on what was offered to them. They accepted Jesus as Lord and as Savior and they claimed the promise of the Holy Spirit. Similarly we can ask ourselves, Have I committed my life to Christ as Lord? Have I consciously claimed by faith the reality of the Holy Spirit in my life? Do I know God's invading presence of love and power in my life?

Let us claim for the first time or reclaim these privileges God longs to give us. Thanks be to God!

Let us root our beliefs and experiences in God's teachings. In the next chapter we will study some "teaching" passages on receiving the Holy Spirit into our lives, and relate these to what we observed in the narrative materials.

CHAPTER 3

God's Plan for Us to Receive the Baptism with the Spirit

In a weekend retreat focusing on the Holy Spirit, a woman shared her experience of coming alive in the Spirit. She experienced peace and joy and the awareness of the Spirit's power and spiritual gifts in her life.

She received her experience in a non-Mennonite setting. While she was happy in her experience, she was sad because she felt Mennonite theology could not accept all she had experienced in the Spirit. When I assured her that in believers church theology one can receive all that God has to offer in the Holy Spirit, she was visibly relieved.

In this chapter we will study the teachings of the Bible on how one receives the baptism with the Spirit and some of the meanings of that phrase. Some suggestions will follow on moving beyond the "definition hassle" in which we talk past each other. These will be from a believers church perspective.

The Promise of the Spirit

To receive the Holy Spirit is to receive the promise God made to all (Acts 2:17, 39). When was the promise made and why? I used to think it began in the upper room with the promise of Jesus to send the Spirit after he was gone. I discovered God had made the promise long before then.

One of the prophets who recorded the promise of the Spirit was Ezekiel, some six centuries before the time of Jesus. Through him God promised a new covenant. In that promise we see the essential elements in Christian experience and the central place of the Holy Spirit.

Salvation Meets the Needs

God speaking through Ezekiel said,

> I will sprinkle clean water on you, and you will be clean; I will cleanse you from all your impurities and from all your idols. I will give you a new heart and put a new spirit in you; I will remove from you your heart of stone and give you a heart of flesh. And I will put my Spirit in you and move you to follow my decrees and be careful to keep my laws. You will live in the land I gave your forefathers; you will be my people, and I will be your God.
>
> (Ezek. 36:25–28, NIV)

God promised a new spirit within, one which would not worship idols. God promised a cleansing from all impurities, the gift of God's Spirit as the source of new motivation and power, and adoption into God's family—a new identity and close relationship as God's people.

Why was all of this necessary? The promises in the new covenant are the remedies, the "medicine" to heal the illness of the people of Israel. God's word through the prophet diagnosed their illness:

> Since you eat meat with the blood still in it and look to your idols and shed blood, should you then possess the land? You rely on your sword, you do detestable things, and each of you defiles his neighbor's wife. Should you then possess the land?" (Ezek. 33:25–26, NIV)

The illness involved serving idols rather than God and relying on the sword rather than the Spirit to resolve conflicts. It was trying to find meaning in relationships through illicit sex rather than in belonging to God's people. Thus they also needed cleansing from these detestable deeds.

We will look at the promises of the covenant and the illnesses they were to heal to see how the New Testament deals with them. I will relate the healing of illnesses and the promises of the covenant primarily to Peter's invitation to the 3000 on the day of Pentecost. I will also make use of some of the teachings of Jesus and Paul to show how they all integrate.

The Basic Elements in Salvation

Peter's invitation to salvation (Acts 2:36–41) *gives us a model to understand what salvation is and a model to use when we invite people to Christ.*

Repent: Confess Jesus is Lord. The three thousand heard Peter's explanation of what God had done through Jesus and that their elders had killed the one God had made both Lord and Christ. They asked, "What shall we do?" Peter responded with his first word, "Repent."

The word *repent* means to change one's mind, to change direction. Their elders had gone against God and chosen their own desires, so they crucified Jesus, their Messiah. Peter said in effect, "Change your minds about Jesus. Let him be Lord and Christ in your lives. Don't you crucify him as your elders did."

The Israelites had chosen their desires and looked to idols and shed blood. They had adopted the Canaanite practice of offering their firstborn to the idols. According to Ezekiel, in the new covenant they would have a new heart, no longer a heart of stone.

Paul wrote that if anyone is in Christ, such a person is

a new creation. To be in Christ is to live no longer for self but for him who died and was raised for us (2 Cor. 5:14–17). It is to become a new creation. Did not Jesus say we must be born again of water and the Spirit (John 3:1–16)? When Jesus called people to be his disciples, he asked them to deny self and follow him (Luke 9:23).

Thus Jesus and Peter and Paul are asking people to decide who is in charge of their lives—self or Christ? "Change your minds and confess Jesus is Lord!" say all three. The self we deny is not our person. It is the self the Bible calls pride, full of the illusions that we are self-made, have enough knowledge to know life's true goals, and have enough resources to cope with life's problems and to reach those goals.

There is only one source of power strong enough to deal with the prideful self and the power of sin. That is the cross of Jesus. In Galatians 6:14, Paul writes that it is through the cross of Christ that the world is crucified (put to death) to him, and he to the world.

In Romans 6:1–18, Paul states that the old self was crucified with Christ to do away with the body of sin. We are to count ourselves dead to sin so we can be servants of God. This is the basis of being able to deny self and confess that Jesus is Lord.

Peter's first word is to let Jesus be Lord in our personal history. The New Testament calls the decision to turn from the false self to Christ a death, for it involves a "loss of face," to use an Oriental expression. Only after such a decision do we find our true self. Yes, repent, change your mind. Confess Jesus is the one who shapes our lives. This answers the question of what or who is the guiding star or who is in charge of our lives. The Holy Spirit brings this change about and applies the finished work of Jesus to our lives. The Spirit leads us to confess, "Jesus is Lord." Thus the Spirit is in our lives.

Baptized for Forgiveness: Jesus Is Savior. Peter's second word involved making the response to the first word public and receiving forgiveness for loving the false self and for the ways in which we have messed up our lives. Peter calls for baptism "in the name of Jesus Christ for the forgiveness of your sins."

Baptism in the first century involved identification with a teacher or movement. Thus baptism involved a public identification with Jesus not only as teacher but also as Lord. "Jesus is Lord, not Caesar" was the confession of the early church.

Baptism also witnesses to cleansing, the forgiveness of the sins which were the fruit of one's living to the false self. Forgiveness deals with the guilt we feel from our failures to live as we know God calls us to live. Forgiveness also deals with our rebellion—our participation in the crucifixion of Jesus—in that we loved the false self more than we loved God.

God promised through Ezekiel, "I will sprinkle clean water on you, and you will be clean; I will cleanse you from all your impurities and from all your idols" (Ezek. 36:25, NIV).

God promised through Peter, "Be baptized . . . in the name of Jesus Christ for the forgiveness of your sins." "In the name of" stands for all the person is and has done. Through the finished work of Jesus, God made provision for our cleansing and forgiveness. Jesus portrayed God as the forgiving father of the prodigal son (Luke 15:11–32). Paul saw God coming in Christ to bring reconciliation and forgiveness (2 Cor. 5:18–21). This answers the question of how one deals with failure in one's life, especially before the eternal Maker. How great is God's mercy! Baptism witnesses to Jesus as our Lord and our Savior.

Receive the Spirit: Jesus Is Baptizer. Peter went on to his third word: "And you will receive the gift of the Holy

Spirit." Peter had told his listeners that what they were seeing and hearing was evidence that Jesus was resurrected, was at the right hand of God, and had received from God the promised Holy Spirit. This was the Spirit promised by Ezekiel and other prophets that would be the central gift in the new covenant. Peter said to his listeners, "This gift is for you."

The promise, however, went beyond Peter's listeners who were several generations of Jewish believers. The promise was also to their children. This was the Hebrew way of speaking of succeeding generations (Ps. 103:17), not speaking about five to ten-year-old children. The promise was also to those who are "far off." While those distant in geography (Rome) and in time (twentieth century) were included, this is not what Peter meant primarily. The "far off" were the Gentiles (see Eph. 2:11–18) who now receive the same covenant blessing as the Jews, God's chosen people. Now the Gentiles are among those "whom the Lord our God will call."

To receive the gift of the Holy Spirit is to receive the baptism with the Spirit, even as Jesus promised his disciples (Acts 1:5; cf. Matt. 3:11). *Jesus is always the Baptizer* and baptizes us with the Holy Spirit. The Spirit starts us on the life and walk in the Spirit through the new birth (discussed above). The Spirit brings us into the body of Christ (discussed in the next section). We receive the Spirit of Christ as God's presence in our lives—our teacher, guide, and comforter.

When the Holy Spirit is poured out upon us we receive power in our lives. Spiritual gifts are released in ministry. (This is the understanding of Jesus regarding the baptism with the Spirit in Acts 1:5, 8.) The Holy Spirit is also God's deposit or down payment in our lives, guaranteeing all the promises of what is to come (2 Cor. 1:20–22).

Peter promises his listeners that they will "receive" the

gift of the Holy Spirit. In the original language, the word for "receive" can mean to grasp hold of, "to take," as in "taking up one's cross" (Matt. 10:38). It can also mean "to accept," to reach out actively and take. To receive corresponds to God's giving: God gives. We receive.

To receive the Holy Spirit into one's life is to answer the question of what is the source of strength enough to cope with anything that may come in life. It is an informed decision by faith, as are the faith decisions to lay hold of Jesus as Lord and as Savior.

Peter simply invites his listeners to confess in baptism that Jesus is both Lord and Savior and to receive the gift of the Holy Spirit.

Identify with God's People: Jesus Is Head. Peter's fourth word not only called for decision, but also for action to identify with God's new people. Luke writes that Peter spoke a long time, warning them and pleading with them to save themselves from the rebellious generation of their elders. Their elders had rejected the Messiah sent for God's people. The words *wicked, evil,* and *corrupt,* which some translations use, may suggest a catalog of evil deeds. The words *perverse* and *untoward* get to the heart of the matter. Their elders were rebellious, for they were going the wrong direction, not going toward God. What was needed was not primarily a new morality, but a new allegiance to God. The new morality should follow. In the light of this, God was establishing a new people.

For the Hebrew reader, the signs of the first Exodus (in which God established the covenant people) were present in the coming of the Holy Spirit on the day of Pentecost. The sound like a mighty wind was like the wind which held back the waters of the Red Sea. The tongues of fire, distributed from a central mass, were like the pillar of fire which led the children of Israel in the wilderness. They were like the fire which descended on the top of the mountain when the law was given. They received the gift of the Spirit which corresponds to the gift of the law upon which the first covenant was formed. The signs pointed toward a second Exodus in which God was forming a new people with a new covenant.

God had promised such a relationship in the new covenant through Ezekiel: "You will be my people and I will be your God." Jesus established the nucleus of the new community when he called the twelve disciples. Larger circles of disciples existed, the 70 for example. On the day of Pentecost there were 120 who gathered, to whom others could be added. Paul wrote that we are baptized with one Spirit into one body, a body with many members who are spiritual gifts to each other (1 Cor. 12:12–31). Thus the body of Christ finds expression in visible congregations around the world.

Let us note briefly three items. One item has to do with the phrase, "baptized by one Spirit into one body." How does this relate to the "baptism with the Spirit?"

The phrase, "baptized with the Holy Spirit," occurs seven times in the New Testament. The construction in the original language is the same in all seven uses. Four are in the Gospels in John's description of the coming ministry of Jesus: "He will baptize with the Holy Spirit."

The fifth and sixth are in Acts 1:5 and 11:16 in which Jesus quotes John the Baptist and then Peter quotes Jesus. In all of these either Jesus (or God) is the baptizer.

The preposition can be translated "in," "with," or "by." In the six uses already noted it is translated "with the Spirit."

With the construction exactly the same, it is difficult to understand why the seventh use (1 Cor. 12:13) is translated "baptized by one Spirit." A basic guide in translation would say it should be the same translation as the others unless there is some strong indication otherwise. Paul writes that all the parts "form one body. So it is with Christ. For we were all baptized by [with] one Spirit into one body" (1 Cor. 12:12–13, NIV). Christ is the major figure, thus the Holy Spirit is the medium of the baptism.

Thus Christ is the Baptizer who baptizes (initiates) us with the medium of the Holy Spirit into his body. By this work through the Spirit, Christ breaks all the barriers that would keep people out of his body. With the Spirit, Christ binds us together in one body. Thus we can say that the baptism with the Spirit has this meaning in addition to the one Jesus gave it in Acts 1:5, 8 where the Spirit comes with power for ministry. In fact, the one helps the other to happen. The Spirit comes upon us with power and fills us with God's love. This in turn enables the breaking of all barriers in the body of Christ and binds us together in one body.

The second item concerns Paul's affirmation of "one Lord, one faith, one baptism" (Eph. 4:5). Paul is concerned about the "oneness" of our faith. How does "one baptism" relate to the "baptism with water" and the "baptism with the Holy Spirit"?

In Paul's life, baptism related to the forgiveness of sins (Acts 22:16), to the fullness of the Spirit (Acts 9:17–18), and to belonging to Christ (1 Cor. 1:12–17). Paul also relates baptism to dying and rising to new life in Christ (Rom. 6:1–11), and to being brought into the body of Christ (Gal. 3:27–28). The inward meanings and the outward rite are intended to be joined in one baptism. For Paul, water baptism is an act of identification with Christ and the fullness of salvation Christ gives when accompanied by faith.

We need to raise the question of whether the use of the plural *baptisms* by the writer of the book of Hebrews means several Christian baptisms, distinguishing between water baptism and the baptism with the Spirit. The word used for *baptisms* in Hebrews 6:2 is not used for water baptism or Spirit baptism anywhere else in the New Testament. The word used is for the ceremonial washing of cups and pots (Matt. 7:4; Mark 7:8), and for various washings (presumably of persons) in the old covenant ceremonial system (Heb. 9:10).

Thus one can hardly say the writer is dealing with several Christian baptisms. "Instruction about baptisms" (washings) appears to contrast Christian baptism with all other religious washings, Jewish and pagan. The writer warns his readers to leave such concerns and to go on to maturity. The instruction about Christian baptism would cover all its meanings, including the baptism with the Spirit.

So there is one body, one Spirit, one hope, one Lord, one faith, one baptism, and one God who is personal and over all relationships (Eph. 4:4–6).

The third item concerns the importance of Peter's fourth element: identify with God's people. Christ knits us with the Spirit into one body composed of people with spiritual gifts who minister to each other. This is the habitat, the living environment, for believers in Christ. Water baptism is the witness of our incorporation into Christ, the head of the church, and thus into his body.

The body of Christ is expressed in visible congregations around the world. The doctrine of the invisible church was the creation of St. Augustine to deal with a state church and infant baptism, the pattern after the fourth century. When he looked out over his congregation in the fifth century and asked, "Where is the true church?" he could only answer, "God only knows."

The church in the New Testament was visible, expressed in congregations around the rim of the Mediterranean Sea. There is no invisible church, except the church of the departed saints. People were baptized into these visible congregations. There was no other way to survive. They needed the ministry of each other's spiritual gifts.

Thus today for us to baptize believers apart from church membership is to confirm them in the illness from which they are to be redeemed, the illness of self-sufficiency and individualism. In this Spirit-filled body, members are to have equal concern for one another (1 Cor. 12:25), a covenant to share each other's sufferings and joys (v. 26), and a readiness to be mutually accountable in fulfilling their commitment to Christ (Matt. 18:15–20).

To disdain a covenant with a congregation of believers is to reject the Spirit's design for surviving as a Christian. The believer's experience with Christ is personal but only partly private. The believer lives as a disciple-in-community. This fourth element answers the question, In what shall I invest my life that gives purpose and will at the same time give me the supportive relationships I need?

Let us return to Peter. Peter invited his hearers to identify with the new people of God. Luke writes that 3,000 were added to their number that day. The invitation to salvation involves identifying with God's visible people in a congregation.

Congregations will need to work at arriving at a good balance between two concerns. On the one hand the witness of baptism should be as close to the conversion experience as possible. On the other, the witness of baptism symbolizes a considered decision to count the cost of Jesus as Lord and to live in a body life of mutual support and counsel. Jesus clearly taught the need to count the cost in following him (e.g., Luke 14:25–35).

Luke and Paul teach the importance of being in a body of believers (Acts 2:41–47; 1 Cor. 12; Rom. 12). The exception of the Ethiopian eunuch should not establish the principle of water baptism at conversion and church membership at some later time. Spirit-led judgment must determine how soon baptism follows conversion.

God's Plan for Us to Receive the Baptism

We now need to face squarely the question of the meaning of the baptism with the Spirit. Let us look at some of the alternatives.

One view focuses on the three words used in Acts for receiving the Spirit. The words *gift* of the Spirit, *receiving* the Spirit, and *baptism* with the Spirit are used interchangeably. Peter uses the three phrases to describe the experience of Cornelius (Acts 10:47; 11:15–17). If *baptism with the Spirit* refers to receiving the Spirit into one's life, then obviously this happens in one's initial reception of the Spirit. This occurs in the new birth, the experience of regeneration (John 3:5; Titus 3:5). Therefore, *baptism with the Spirit* is synonymous with the new birth. The Spirit comes inwardly and quietly without the believer's decision or awareness. Furthermore, there is no emphasis on receiving the Spirit as power as part of the conversion experience. The *logic* of the words in Acts is related to some of the teaching materials in the New Testament to arrive at this meaning. *Logic* seems to prevail in this first view.

A second alternative uses the phrase *baptism with the Spirit* as an umbrella term to cover the whole of the conversion experience. This view recognizes baptism with the Spirit as initiation into the life in the Spirit, the new covenant. The elements in the conversion experience are the four elements in Peter's invitation on the day of Pentecost, the four elements in Ezekiel's promise of the new covenant. The Spirit is involved in all four of them. This includes receiving the Holy Spirit as power for ministry as one of the significant parts of conversion. The promises of Jesus that his disciples would be baptized with the Spirit (Acts 1:4–5) and that when power comes upon them they would be his witnesses (Acts 1:8) are closely connected. To define *baptism with the Spirit* without reference to these statements of Jesus is incredulous.

A third view defines *baptism with the Spirit* almost totally by Acts 1:4–5, and 8 where the Holy Spirit as power comes upon the disciples to make them witnesses of Christ and to carry out his ministry. This view affirms that the Holy Spirit is active in the other elements in conversion. However, the term *baptism with the Spirit* is defined by Acts 1:8. If we follow the instances of receiving the Spirit in Acts, we see that it does not happen without the believer's awareness. To receive the gift of the Spirit is to actively lay hold of the promise of the Spirit and to experience the power of the Spirit in witnessing for Christ. In most of the conversion experiences in Acts, the awareness of the Spirit as power was present.

Some who hold the third view believe the baptism with the Spirit occurs sometime after conversion. However, our study has shown that throughout Acts, persons received the baptism with the Spirit when they became new covenant believers. The only exceptions are the 120 and the Samaritans. I have noted the reasons which exclude them from being the normative pattern. Thus I believe it is God's intention that we experience the baptism with the Spirit at our conversion, whether one holds view 2 or view 3. (View 1 already holds this position but defines it differently.)

Aside from the exegetical problems with view 1, its results in the life of the church have not been encouraging. John R. W. Stott who holds view 1, writes that the church in the West has largely lost the Christian faith as well as the Christian ethic. "The dead, dry bones of the church need the living breath of God" (*Baptism and Fulness*, p. 13). I have little hope that view 1 will revive the church.

I do not know if view 2 can keep enough focus on the Holy Spirit as the power in personal and congregational life by using the phrase "baptism with the Spirit" for the whole experience. It is the most faithful to the New Testament in that it recognizes the interchangeble use of *gift, receive,* and *baptism with the Spirit* in Acts in beginning the Christian life. It also relates the baptism with the Spirit with power for ministry as in Acts 1:8. It does not fall off either end of the issue in the book of Acts. Furthermore, it is in keeping with teachings on the Holy Spirit in other books.

I am sympathetic to those who hold view 3. They have a strong desire to renew a weak and struggling church. In this book, I am highlighting the meaning of view 3 in the phrase, *the baptism with the Spirit,* though one could set it in the context of the larger framework of view 2. I cannot deny that in three quarters of a century the combined forces of the Pentecostals and the charismatics have become between 15 and 20 percent of the total Christian church. While there are divergent theologies among them, God has clearly used them. I rejoice that Christ is preached and the Spirit is given freedom to work. They honor the Spirit and worship the Son.

Could we also honor the Spirit and worship the Son by affirming the following statements?

First, *the Spirit is calling us away from our idolatries and self-sufficiency* to give allegiance to Christ.

Second, in our submission to Christ *God can pour out the Holy Spirit into our lives,* regardless of differences in our views on how that happens.

Third, *only by the power of the Spirit can any of us minister.* Only by that power can the church come alive and be witnesses for Christ.

With these affirmations we can love and trust each other, worship and work together, while we seek the mind of the Spirit on how to jointly express our faith.

The Spirit as the Central Gift

Jesus expected that those who became believers in him would experience the Holy Spirit as an indwelling presence and power. This would result in blessings flowing through them to others (John 7:37–39; Acts 1:8).

The Jewish people prayed for the Messiah and his kingdom to come. With that would come many blessings. Matthew records one teaching of Jesus about prayer that is instructive here. Jesus says that while earthly parents are evil (selfish) and yet give good gifts to their children, much more will God give good gifts to those who ask him (Matt. 7:11). Rabbis used the phrase *good gifts* to speak of the height of blessings in the new kingdom. In a parallel passage, Luke writes, "How much more will your Father in heaven give the Holy Spirit to those who ask him" (Luke 11:13, NIV). Apparently Jesus saw the Holy Spirit as the highest gift in becoming a new covenant believer, one of which the believer would have awareness.

Why did Jesus say, "keep on asking," using the present tense? Does this mean God does not give the Spirit in conversion and that one needs to keep on asking until one finally receives? This does not square with Peter's invitation to the 3000 or with what we saw was Paul's expectation in Acts 19 and Galatians 3, so we conclude not.

Another view is that it involves a succession of persons—but always a different person—coming and continuously asking and receiving. This is certainly the hope of all who want new people to come to salvation.

A third view is that Jesus saw believers coming in prayer (the context of the promise) again and again with awareness of their need for God's empowering. The believers who were baptized with the Spirit at Pentecost and were filled, cried out to God again for empowering to witness. And they were filled again (Acts 4:23–31). So it is appropriate for Christians to sing as a prayer, "Spirit of the living God, fall afresh on me (on us)."

When Paul taught the Galatians how to become people with right relationships with God through faith, he saw the central gift of God's total redemptive plan to be the gift of the Holy Spirit. God "redeemed us in order that the blessing given to Abraham might come to the Gentiles through Christ Jesus, so that by faith we might receive the promise of the Spirit" (Gal. 3:14, NIV). Paul expected believers would receive the Holy Spirit when they believed in Christ. They would be aware that they had received the Spirit (Acts 19:2, 5–6).

In summary, the narrative materials in Acts and the teaching materials in the New Testament all point to God's intention that we receive the baptism with the Holy Spirit at the same time we confess Jesus as our Lord and Savior. At that time we are to receive by faith the presence and power of the Holy Spirit in our lives as part of that experience. We are also to identify with a congregation of God's people. *These four informed intentional decisions constitute the salvation experience.*

The person who has experienced these four elements of the gospel is a babe in Christ. A personal renewal experience does not change the level of one's maturity. It only opens the door to resources.

Growth through personal disciplines in the Scriptures and prayer, receiving teachings, following mentors, participating in corporate worship and a support group, experiencing struggles and hardships, and participating in witnessing and various ministries will follow.

Growth to maturity and discovery of the implications of each of the four areas are unending. However, one begins as a babe with an understanding of the nucleus of each of the four elements in Peter's invitation. They are the doorway into the path of following Christ. Baptism witnesses to this entrance.

Faith Dramas Witnessing to Salvation

Baptism. The fullness of this salvation experience is witnessed in baptism, a drama which is to stimulate our faith in the realities to which it points us:

1. Dying to self (idols) and rising to new life (heart) in Christ. Identifying with Christ and confessing that he is Lord (Rom. 6:1–11; Acts 2:36–38). Jesus is Lord.
2. Cleansing from sin and being reconciled with God (Acts 2:38; 22:16). Jesus is Savior.
3. Pouring out the Holy Spirit into one's life for joyful motivation to do God's will, for power to love the unlovely, and for power in daily living and witnessing (Acts 1:8; 2:38–39; 10:44–48). Jesus is the Baptizer.
4. Coming into the visible body of Christ of which Christ is the head, entering into mutual nurture and care and accountability (Acts 2:40–47; 1 Cor. 12:12–27). Jesus is the Head.
5. Accepting our calling to witness, enabled by the power and gifts of the Holy Spirit with Jesus as our example (Matt. 3:13–17; 4:18–23; Eph. 4:7–16). Jesus is the ascended King.

Baptism witnesses to our entering by faith into the new covenant with Christ and his people. *Baptism is the covenant made.*

Communion. Whenever we participate in communion, we renew our baptismal covenant. In communion, the new covenant meal:

1. We reaffirm Christ's lordship and our commitment to him (1 Cor. 11:23–26).
2. We reaffirm Christ's sacrifice for us which offers forgiveness, cleansing, and reconciliation with God. We reaffirm that we live by continuing grace (Matt. 26:26–29).

3. We reaffirm our drinking the one Spirit of the new covenant (1 Cor. 12:13).
4. We reaffirm our being bound together in one body (1 Cor. 10:16–17; 11:18–34; 12:12–27).
5. We reaffirm that we proclaim the new covenant until Christ comes (1 Cor. 11:26).

Thus we can say that communion is the covenant reaffirmed.

The narrative materials, the teachings of Jesus, Peter, and Paul, and the witness of baptism and communion—all speak to the fullness of the salvation we receive. Thus we conclude that the fullness of the salvation is seen as the "remedy" for our "illnesses." The tendency to love our false self (idols) more than God is met by the new love of Jesus as Lord. Our failures (sins) in being what we could be are met by the healing of forgiveness and restored relationships. Our inner weakness and lack of motivation to do what we know we ought is met by the gracious indwelling of the Holy Spirit as God's love and power in our lives. Our search for meaning in relationships and for something worth investing our lives in is satisfied by the new community of God's people. How great is God's salvation toward those who choose to reverence God!

I have often been asked, "Why do many people experience the baptism with the Spirit as a second major experience some time after their conversion, if it is God's intention that it should happen at conversion?" That is a good question. We will examine it in the next chapter.

CHAPTER 4

The Variety of Experiences Today

In the past several decades, millions of Christians around the world have experienced what is called the "baptism with the Spirit." For many, this has been a second major experience in their lives. If it is God's plan for believers to receive the baptism with the Spirit at the time of their conversion, how does one explain this?

Of course, many do receive the baptism with the Spirit as a part of their conversion experience, as Peter promised to the 3000 on the day of Pentecost. Thus if one says that a subsequent major experience is the norm (God's intention, which I do not hold), then one has to say the 3000 were an exception—not to mention Paul, Cornelius, and the twelve at Ephesus.

We will look at five reasons why there is a variety of experiences in relation to receiving the baptism with the Spirit. We will then examine the relation of the baptism with the Spirit to the fullness of the Spirit. The chapter will conclude with a suggested focus for conversation between believers with differing experiences so they can rejoice together and avoid unnecessary conflict.

Reasons for a Variety of Experiences

Experience to the Extent We Are Taught. One reason for a variety of experiences in receiving the baptism with the

Spirit is that we normally experience to the extent we are taught.

In one weekend workshop on the Holy Spirit, I encouraged people to follow Peter's model when inviting persons to Jesus Christ. One man reported that he did not do that. He helped people find Christ as Lord and Savior as the first experience. A month or more later they would return, defeated and weak in their Christian walk. He would then teach them about the Spirit and help them to experience the baptism with the Spirit.

He was doing what Paul did not do. He was teaching people only part of the salvation experience at one time and the rest at a later time. The classic biblical example of experiencing to the extent one is taught is the group of disciples Paul met at Ephesus (Acts 19:1–7).

These disciples had been taught by Apollos who at that time knew only the baptism of John, a baptism of preparation for the coming Messiah. Under Paul's ministry, these disciples of John learned of the Lord Jesus. What John had promised had come. The Spirit was now available to be given. When Paul baptized them and laid his hands on them, they received the Holy Spirit.

These disciples were taught Old Testament understandings and their experience was in line with these teachings. When they were taught New Testament understandings, then they became Christians. Else why did Paul rebaptize them?

With the rise of science and technology, the felt need for the supernatural declined for a time in the Western world. Relying on the Holy Spirit was not seen as so necessary. Thus many church members have not been pointed to the Holy Spirit as an indwelling presence and power which could be a daily reality in their lives.

With the failure of science and technology to meet the deep inner hungers of life, there has been a searching on the part of many persons for something more. When introduced to the Holy Spirit as a possible present reality in their lives, they reach out in faith in response to the teaching. They experience the baptism with the Spirit. They experience to the extent they are taught.

Another example of persons experiencing as far as they have been taught and not knowing the reality of the Holy Spirit in their lives is that of persons who have been introduced to a truncated or partial gospel. They have understood salvation as the forgiveness of sins. Many of these persons have not been led to experience Jesus as Lord of their lives or to claim the gift of the Holy Spirit as God's presence and power in their lives. The Holy Spirit has been in their lives but able to work only in a limited way.

John Wesley was a priest in the Church of England in the 1700s. He knew the relationship of forgiveness with God but he did not know how to find holiness. Out of his long search he developed a two-stage theology of Christian experience.

The first stage is conversion in which one experiences the forgiveness of sins. Dealing with guilt is the central concern of this stage. In the second stage one experiences what Wesley called "Christian perfection." The central focus of this stage is dealing with the sin nature, or as Wesley called it, the "residue of sin." In this second stage, one receives the Holy Spirit. Some groups today call this experience sanctification or the second blessing. In the hymn, "Rock of Ages," we sing this theology: "Be of sin the *double cure,* save from wrath (guilt), and make me pure (sin nature)."

Wesley's theology, often called holiness theology, led to considerable controversy in the nineteenth and the first half of the twentieth centuries in North America. The Methodist Church disowned the two-stage theology in the 1890s when the church decided that the view discredited the finished work of Christ on the cross.

The two-stage view of Christian experience opened the door for modern Pentecostalism to emerge in 1906 in Los Angeles. From there it has spread around the world. Since it was the second stage which seemed to cause the controversy, the first stage became the focus in the Modernist-Fundamentalist tension. Fundamentalists have emphasized salvation as the forgiveness of sins, and, in effect, left to the denominations the matter of how to deal with sanctification.

As a result many pastors, evangelists, and child evangelism workers have called persons to know Jesus as their Savior. This involves being "born again" and having their sins forgiven. These individuals usually become church members without being taught or experiencing Jesus as Lord or experiencing the gift of the Spirit as God's presence and power in their lives. They experience as far as they have been taught. They do not know Jesus as Lord or Jesus as Baptizer. When they learn about Jesus as Lord and the baptism with the Spirit and respond with hunger and faith, they experience these realities in their lives. They enter into the rest of what Peter offered his hearers in their initial experience with Jesus Christ (see chapter 3).

Congregations need to take responsibility for the gospel they are presenting to others. This is true for parents, pastors, elders, deacons, Sunday school teachers, and youth sponsors. In one sense, the renewal movement is filling the emptiness which occurred because many denominations, including Mennonite, had an inadequate view of the gospel. The church can repent and return to presenting a full gospel. We need to give Peter's full invitation when we present the gospel to a person.

The question often arises then, how shall we respond to children? When a child (any age prepuberty) says to a parent or Sunday school teacher, "I want to be saved" (or become a Christian, or be baptized, or take communion), how shall we respond? Many parents and teachers and pastors respond by reading adult meanings into those words. They do not take time to understand the child's needs; they assume what those needs are. They proceed to make plans for instruction and baptism.

Space in this study permits only a brief treatment of the basic considerations in helping such a child. The first step is to affirm the child in wanting to love Jesus and wanting to belong to the church. "We are glad you want to love Jesus."

The second step is to find out the child's sense of need by asking questions which cannot be answered by yes or no. "Tell me, please, why you want to be saved" (or baptized, or be a Christian). Several more questions may be needed until they share their inner need. Usually the need is one of dealing with guilt for bad deeds. If one asks the child why he or she did the bad deeds, there will often be a shrug of the shoulders and the response, "I don't know, I just did."

The third step is to help meet the child's need. If the child has done bad things and wants Jesus to forgive, help the child ask for forgiveness and assure the child that Jesus has forgiven. Parents and others will need to help children deal with guilt and forgiveness again and again, from little on up. They need to be told that baptism involves more than the forgiveness of sins. They need to learn that when they are older the Holy Spirit will help them understand their sinfulness in a different way. Until that time they belong to Jesus.

If the young person gives evidence of knowing the struggle of the self over against God, then the youth may be struggling with the decision for conversion. One should help the individual accordingly, inviting the person to

Christ with Peter's fourfold invitation.

The child may come out of wanting to belong by participating in the important faith dramas of the congregation—baptism and/or communion. Congregations need to include children in worship and in fellowship activities so they know that they are wanted and that they belong. They need to be assured that they belong without participating in the faith dramas. When they are older and experience the realities toward which baptism and communion point, they can then participate in them.

There are other needs which children may reflect, but for here these will suffice to illustrate how to minister to the needs of children. There are two other crucial considerations. One consideration has to do with the child's relation to God before the first acknowledgment of bad deeds and guilt, at whatever age that happens. Is the child saved or lost?

Parents and pastors have four historic options. One is to believe that the right clergy and the right water result in baptismal regeneration of the infant who is then saved (Roman Catholic). A second option is to believe that the proxy faith of the parents or godparents at the time of baptism saves the child (Lutheran). A third option is to view the child of Christian parents as already in the people of God. Baptism parallels circumcision in the Old Testament as the sign that that is the case (Reformed).

A fourth option (Anabaptist) is to view children as safe in God's grace by God's choice. Youth and adults who choose to believe are saved likewise by God's grace, for we are capable of making the choice as the Holy Spirit reveals our sinfulness to us.

All of this is possible because of Christ's finished work for us. As wide as the illness is, so wide is the remedy Paul describes in Romans 5:12–21. The covenant of Christ's cross covers all children, not just those of Christian parents. Children are already in the kingdom, according to Jesus in Matthew 19:13–14. They are innocent not because they do no wrong, but because they are not accountable before God.

The decision that moves the growing person out of grace is the repeated choice over time to focus in the prideful self rather than God. It is to choose to live by one's own sufficiency and to plan life after one's own interests. It is not to acknowledge God as God, nor to be thankful to God (Rom. 1:18–21). This self is full of pride, for it is saying that I am my own source (creator). I have my own strength (sustainer). I know the goals in life worth living for (destiny). And if there are any failures I can surmount them (savior).

This exposes the true nature of sinfulness. Youth growing up in Christian homes who are taught to be good and respectable often say that in becoming a church member there was no change, not much to it. Is it because we view salvation as forgiveness of bad deeds? Is it because we give prominence to the person who is saved after committing the whole catalog of sins? Sometimes this prominence causes youth from Christian homes to think their experience is inferior because they can't give such a testimony. We need to help youth to see that the prideful self puts Christ on the cross. The sinful self out of which comes self-sufficient and selfish living is no better than the sinful self out of which come deeds destructive to the body and the personality. Both put Christ on the cross and both need the mercy of God. Experiencing the mercy of God becomes a large motivation in joyous worship and in self-giving service to God (Rom. 12:1–2).

This last paragraph raises a second consideration about the relation of children to the gospel and God. At what stage in development can a person experience the self over against God? Jesus said, "If anyone would come after me, he must deny himself and take up his cross daily and follow me" (Luke 9:23). Such a decision involves the capacity of abstract thinking which emerges in puberty (early adolescence). The struggle for mastery over the drives of the body (which are good) underscores the need for strength beyond oneself. The question of whether one lives for self or for God raises the issue of whether Christ is Lord. These are experiences of the adolescent, not the child, which accompany the call of Jesus.

Children will have many religious experiences as they grow in God's love and experience forgiveness. They need to be encouraged to continue loving Jesus. Congregations need to find ways to help them know they belong without inviting children to participate in the faith dramas (baptism and communion) which point to realities which they are unable to experience.

Experience to the Extent of Admitted Need. People also experience to the extent they are ready to admit need. It is possible to resist the idea that one needs the Holy Spirit as power in one's life. One can live by the energy of the "flesh" (the prideful self), seeking to live by one's own strength. The opposite is to acknowledge need and seek what God has to offer, as Cornelius did (Acts 10).

In most churches in North America there are acceptable crutches to keep one from confessing one's deeper need. Respectable behavior usually keeps one acceptable in most congregations. Formal education and training provide a basis for doing work in congregational programs. Organizational knowledge and skills keep the formal operation of the congregation going. In such a context, to confess a deeper spiritual need puts one out of step with others. One becomes the odd person. So it is easier not to confess the deeper need and to keep on living the mediocre Christian life.

Experience According to a Congregation's Expectations. A

third reason there is a variety of experiences in receiving the baptism with the Spirit stems from the spiritual expectations a congregation has. If a congregation does not expect one to experience the Holy Spirit as a reality when meeting Christ, it is not likely that many persons will have such an experience. If the congregation resists the use of certain gifts in congregational life, there will not likely be an openness to the Spirit who is the giver of these gifts.

Paul asks the Galatians whether, having begun the Christian life by faith, they expect to continue by living on their own strength (Gal. 3:1–5). Paul asks them whether God gives the Spirit and does miracles among them because they deserve them or because they believe the promises they heard? Do our congregations expect God to give the Spirit and do miracles among them at all? Members' expectations condition congregational life and affect their relation to God. These expectations may even limit God's action among the members. Their expectations affect how they introduce others to Christ and what is expected in that experience.

Experience According to Congregation's Spiritual Vitality. A fourth reason for a variety of experiences in receiving the baptism with the Spirit is closely related to the third reason. The level of spiritual vitality in the congregation tends to condition people's spiritual experiences. A congregation with little sense of walking in the Spirit, of eagerly seeking the gifts of the Spirit, and with little sense of the Spirit moving in worship will not likely motivate people to search for the life in the Spirit.

Someone who comes alive in the Spirit outside the congregation may return to his or her congregation full of joy and peace in the Spirit. That person may then say, "You are dead. There is no life here." Although that judgment may be harsher than it should be, there may also be some truth in it. I urge congregations to be open to that possibility. Some soul searching before God may be the desire of the Spirit for us both as individuals and as congregations.

Experience as Far as One Lays Hold of God's Promises. A fifth reason for a variety of experiences in receiving the baptism with the Spirit is the extent to which one appropriates God's promises, insofar as the promise rests only on our response. One can be taught and understand the full breadth of the gospel, but not reach out and lay hold of the promise of the presence and power of the Spirit in one's life. One may resist yielding one's life to the control of the Spirit. A person may find it painful to confess that he or she is not self-sufficient. One may resist the searchlight of the Spirit on some selfishly satisfying behaviors that one is not ready to give up. A person may fear that God will give a spiritual gift he or she does not want. Whatever the reason, one may intentionally resist cashing in on God's promise of the gift of the Holy Spirit as a conscious reality in one's life.

A young woman came for help with her spiritual life. It was like a desert. She had no sense of a personal relation to God. Together we sought for the cause, reviewing her spiritual pilgrimage and her faith understandings. We explored her relationships with people in her life. At the end of several conversations she seemed at the verge of yielding her life to the lordship of Christ and claiming the promised gift of the Spirit. Yet she was not quite ready.

After some months she returned. She stated that she feared God would do too much in her life. "Do too much!" I exclaimed, not able to contain my surprise. "Most people want all God wants to give."

"Yes," she said, "I fear God will work too miraculously." "And what is the miracle?" I asked. "I'm afraid I may receive the gift of tongues."

We talked about her fears, about the nature of tongues,

and about God being the gracious giver of every good and perfect gift. She surrendered her life to Jesus as Lord and claimed the promised gift of the Spirit. Nearly a year later she wrote that her spiritual life was vital and meaningful. She added, "And I still have not received the gift of tongues."

Now there are times when experience may go ahead of understanding. Only later the person may find others who can interpret what happened and one comes to the "aha!" At times the experience may be sufficiently different from those of the leaders of the congregation that they may not be able to help understand it. In this situation there needs to be mutual respect and efforts made to find mutually trusted persons who can aid in reaching understanding.

Two Questions

While there are likely additional reasons for the variety of experiences in receiving the baptism with the Holy Spirit, we will deal now with two more questions. The one is: Since some people experience the baptism with the Spirit as a second major experience following conversion, what does one teach others to expect in their experience?

In the light of our studies in chapters 2 and 3, one does not need to develop a two-stage view of Christian experience as in classic Pentecostalism. The invitation to make an informed decision on receiving the Spirit as God's presence and power in one's life was there when one met Christ. One may lay hold of that promise sometime later, but it was there (available) at the time of conversion. It simply was not activated. Now one can claim and experience the promise. New persons coming to Christ can claim it all at conversion and do not need to expect a two-stage experience. The baptism with the Spirit need not follow conversion and water baptism as a subsequent experience. We teach the four elements of Peter's invitation to Christ so new believers can immediately claim the baptism with the Spirit in their conversion.

The second question is how one views earlier spiritual decisions in the light of a new major decision which seems to put all earlier decisions in a shadow. To some, the new decision seems to discredit all previous decisions. The temptation is to say they are not valid; only this new one is valid.

The major impact caused by experiencing a spiritual truth need not discredit previous spiritual decisions. Instead, we simply thank God for each decision as a work of God's grace in our lives, recognizing that we will yet face even more decisions.

The Fullness of the Spirit

This brings us to another question. What is the fullness of the Spirit? What is the relation of the baptism with the Spirit to the fullness of the Spirit?

Jesus told the disciples, "In a few days you will be baptized with the Holy Spirit" (Acts 1:5, NIV). Baptism with the Spirit is the initial experience of the Holy Spirit as power in one's life. The result is that one is filled with the Spirit. Luke writes that on the day of Pentecost "all of them were filled with the Holy Spirit" (Acts 2:4, NIV).

In Acts 4:31 Luke writes these same apostles "were all filled with the Holy Spirit and spoke the word of God boldly" (NIV). Why did the apostles need to be refilled? Had they "leaked"? Did they receive only part of the Spirit the first time? The answer to these questions is "No!"

The clue to these questions appears in the phrase, "and [they] spoke the word of God boldly." The context tells us Peter and John had healed the lame man. They had been imprisoned for proclaiming in Jesus the resurrection of the dead and had been threatened. They were commanded not to "speak or teach at all in the name of Jesus."

The issue clearly was whether they should fear the threats of the rulers and become an underground church, or whether they should continue to give the message of Jesus publicly. The latter would take a lot of courage. In their prayer which followed (Acts 4:24–30), they clearly reaffirmed Jesus as Lord and asked for enabling to speak boldly. God answered their prayer. They experienced again the fullness of the Spirit and spoke the word of God boldly.

Fullness of the Spirit and speaking the word of God boldly are clearly related. In every instance in Acts where Luke reports people were filled with the Spirit, some manner of speaking the word boldly follows. This correlates directly with the words of Jesus to his disciples that they would do greater things than he because he goes to the Father and would send the Spirit of truth (John 14:12–17). After telling the disciples that they would be baptized with the Spirit, Jesus stated, "You will receive power when the Holy Spirit comes on you; and you will be my witnesses" (Acts 1:5–8 NIV). The primary meaning of the baptism with the Spirit is empowerment to witness.

The word *filled* suggests a container. Perhaps more appropriate is the picture of sails filled with the wind. When the sails are filled, the boat is empowered to action. When the sails are empty, there is deadness, no action. When fullness comes, things happen which could not otherwise happen. Even with all of the church's problems, Luke's description in the book of Acts shows a church empowered to witness.

The issue in coming to Christ in salvation is who is in charge. Is it we or the Lord? By what power will we live, by our own or by God's power in the Spirit? We confront these same issues anew whenever we face an area of our lives not yielded to Christ or when we are tempted to return to self-centered living. Yielding ourselves anew to

Christ's lordship and claiming again the presence and power of the Spirit result in being filled anew with the Spirit, with an empowerment to witness.

The context of Ephesians 5:18 has to do with value choices and following the Lord's will. Paul used the verb tense of continuing action, "Keep on being filled with the Spirit." As we behold the person of Christ, the Spirit will show us areas of our lives not like Christ's life. As we yield these areas, the Spirit changes us from one degree of likeness to Christ to another (2 Cor. 3:17–18). This is "keeping on being filled with the Spirit."

The Holy Spirit is a person; we do not receive parts of the Spirit. Rather we are released from the prideful self into the image of Christ. The Spirit receives more and more of us as we read the Scriptures, heed the counsel of brothers and sisters in Christ, and are sensitive to the Spirit's voice within. There is one baptism with the Spirit and many infillings with the Spirit.

Sometimes people ask, "Isn't the charismatic experience simply a deeper spiritual experience in which one experiences a new fullness of the Spirit?" If one holds that the new birth (confessing Jesus is Lord) and the baptism with the Spirit are synonymous, then one would need to conclude that. If they are not synonymous, as our study has shown, then laying hold of the reality of the Holy Spirit as God's presence and power in one's life needs a first-time decision. This is similar to the need to confess Jesus as Lord and as Savior in first-time decisions. Thus for many persons, the charismatic experience is dealing with a deficiency in their conversion experience. It is not simply a new "being filled with the Spirit," though being filled with the Spirit is a result. It is the initial claiming of the promise of the presence and power of the Holy Spirit in their lives.

Summary of Views

Let us review again in a different formulation the range of views concerning the baptism with the Spirit. We can arrange them along a continuum. Some of the views are as follows.

View 1. At one end of the continuum is the view that one receives the gift of the Spirit in the new birth. This is another way of talking about the baptism with the Spirit. They are synonymous. The gift of the Spirit comes silently as an inner work. The believer need not be aware of it. One's focus is on Christ, not on the Holy Spirit. The gift of speaking in tongues is not involved or expected. One grows in one's awareness of the person and ministry of the Spirit.

View 2. Next along the continuum, is the view that the Holy Spirit is present throughout the experience of becoming a Christian. Without the Spirit no part of it would be possible. The Spirit enables the believer to confess by faith that Jesus is Lord and Savior. The gift of the Spirit (the baptism with the Spirit) is the believer receiving by faith the reality of the presence of the Spirit in one's life and the Spirit as power for witnessing. One may or may not speak in tongues. The decision to receive the Spirit by faith is one of the decisions made in the total experience called conversion. This is when God intends the baptism with the Spirit to occur. There is a growth in understanding the person and ministry of the Spirit.

View 3. The next stop on the continuum is actually an exception or addition to the second view. If for some reason one did not claim the Holy Spirit as God's presence and power in one's life at conversion, one can make such a claim later and joyfully experience the baptism with the

Spirit. One may or may not speak in tongues. One can recognize that the baptism with the Spirit was available at conversion, but for some reason was not claimed. One can read the experience back into conversion as an essential part of what God planned for that time. Growth in understanding the person and ministry of the Spirit follows.

View 4. Proceeding along the continuum we come to the view that first one becomes a Christian through the new birth and the forgiveness of sins. Normally, it is sometime later that one has a second major experience; one receives the baptism with the Spirit. One may or may not speak in tongues. Growth in understanding the person and ministry of the Spirit follows.

View 5. At the other end of the continuum is a view similar to view 4, except that speaking in tongues *must* accompany the baptism with the Spirit. If one does not speak in tongues, one has not received the baptism with the Spirit.

The reader will recognize that views 2 and 3 have been the conclusion of the biblical study in this booklet. Others may reach other conclusions.

The Statement on "The Holy Spirit in the Life of the Church" (Mennonite General Assembly, 1977) recognizes the above conclusions. It states that "the New Testament use of the language of being baptized with the Spirit is either in relation to the original event at Pentecost or subsequently to the bestowal of the Spirit at the time of conversion."

The statement goes on to note that "more significant than the terminology is the experience which the language is meant to describe." The document describes the experiences of the New Testament and the "fresh and transforming experiences in relationship to the Spirit." It examines some reasons for the variety of experiences.

The significant statements for our study then follow. "The experience of conversion for many people in our times has lacked the full meaning that it seemed to have in apostolic times. In this context God is honoring the phrase 'the baptism in the Spirit' to help many people appropriate more fully what he intended at conversion. Although there are problems in using the phrase in this way we recognize that it can be helpful in ministering to persons."

Two items are of particular note. One is that many people are lacking something in Christian experience that was present in apostolic times. Ministering the "baptism in the Spirit" is being honored today by God to help people experience what God intended in conversion. This is in line with views 2 and 3 above.

The second item is that this use of "the baptism in the Spirit" (helping people to appropriate more fully what God intended at conversion) does cause problems. It makes a problem for those who hold that the gift of the Spirit and the baptism with the Spirit are synonymous with the new birth. For those who believe the baptism with the Spirit, while not synonymous with the new birth, is to occur in conversion, this use does make an exception. To use the phrase, "the baptism with the Spirit," to help people appropriate what God intended at conversion makes a problem for those who believe the baptism with the Spirit always follows conversion. Is experiencing the reality of the Spirit sometime after conversion a strategy of the Spirit in our day to call the church to a greater recognition of the need to appropriate the Holy Spirit at the time of conversion? I believe it may be.

These paragraphs also raise the question of how we accept each other when we differ. I want to offer some suggestions.

Accepting Differing Experiences

Let us return to our imagined meeting of Cornelius and Manasses at Jacob's well.

Cornelius: You seem very happy.
Manasses: Oh, yes. We had great events that changed my life.
Cornelius: Changed your life? Tell me about it.
Manasses: Philip preached that the Messiah had come. We received the message with joy. Peter and John came from Jerusalem some weeks later and we received the Holy Spirit.
Cornelius: Peter came to my house and I received Christ and the Holy Spirit all at one time. I was saved.

(Acts 10:34–48; 11:14–17)

How might the conversation end?

Option 1:

Manasses: But one always receives the baptism with the Spirit as a second experience. I know because that is the way my experience was. You don't have the baptism with the Spirit.
Cornelius: I received the same Spirit. One receives the baptism with the Spirit at conversion. Why do you have to discredit my experience because it was not like yours?

Option 2:

Manasses: I am glad you are saved. When the Spirit came into my life I found I could love the Jews who called us foolish. I experience the joy and peace of God in my life whether I have money or I am broke. I have courage to witness for Christ, and the Spirit gives me the gifts I need to do that.

Cornelius: Praise the Lord. The ways we were saved and received the Spirit were certainly different but we are certainly brothers in the same family when it comes to what the Spirit is doing in our lives. I am experiencing the same working of the Spirit.

Let us return to real life. Let us confess that we often judge the experience of other people. We ask, was it right (the same as ours) or not?

When we talk with people whose experience with the Spirit differs from ours, let us begin by focusing on the results of our experience with the Lord. We know ourselves as God's children with a trusting, intimate relationship with God (Rom. 8:15–17). The Scriptures come alive for us (Acts 2:41). We experience God's leading (Rom. 8:14). We have joy and peace and concern for justice and wholeness (Rom. 14:17). We experience the Holy Spirit enabling our prayers and praying through us (Rom. 8:26–27). We experience growth in the fruit of the Spirit in being able to love even our enemies (Rom. 5:5–10; Gal. 5:22–23). We have joy in worshiping God and fellowshiping with God's people (Acts 2:41–46; Eph. 5:18–20). And we receive one or more spiritual gifts and the empowering of the Spirit to use them to build the body of Christ and to witness to the good news (1 Cor. 12:7, Acts 1:8).

After the Spirit binds us together in common experiences in Christ, we may seek to understand the path of our experiences in the light of our differing understandings of the Scriptures. We may find we can accept each other's experiences without needing to insist that everyone's must be like ours. Hopefully, our theology will become broader than our own experience.

As persons with differing experiences work at the above tasks, we can exercise patience. We can learn to sit where the other persons sit *before* we ask whether they are right or wrong. Only then will we know what we are evaluating.

To do this we will need to agree that each person will get equal time to express his or her experiences and views. During this sharing, the other person will put into his or her own words what is being heard and then ask, "Have I heard you right?" Questions and "Yes, but's" are not permitted in this stage.

After each person's views and feelings have been expressed and understood, the persons first note areas of agreement. Then areas of differences can be noted.

Those differences which can benefit by further work can be examined *one at a time*. Clarifying views and getting further information may help. A third party to help communication is often helpful.

In congregations we can say to each other, "Yes, we affirm the presence of the Holy Spirit in the Christian life. We will affirm your experience and expect you to affirm ours. We will study, share, pray, and learn from each other.

"Yes, we believe it is only by the power of the Holy Spirit that one can live the Christian life and the work of the church can go forward. We want to study and pray together on how the Spirit works, expecting some changes in our personal and congregational life.

"Yes, we believe the Holy Spirit aids us in worship. We want worship to be alive and meaningful, using our person in action and in silence. We will affirm some of the things which are meaningful to you if you will affirm some of the things that are meaningful to us. We will make changes gradually, committed to accepting changes.

"Yes, we believe the Spirit gives spiritual gifts in great diversity. There are some in the New Testament which we are not used to in our church life and there may be some today not named in the New Testament. We will enlarge our understandings of these gifts to overcome any fear and to learn appropriate ways and places for all of them to be expressed.

"Yes, we do hold our beliefs quite firmly. We become emotionally attached to the way we have always done things. We find it hard to change. We know we are brothers and sisters in Christ and that the Spirit brings change. Please don't push us too hard and we will not push you too hard. We do confess we need some pushing to keep us all from being boxed in by our own expectations."

When we can commit ourselves with such understandings, we discover that love, the fruit of the Spirit, enables us to live together and to affirm each other. Such love becomes the context to release spiritual gifts in caring ministry. In the next chapter we will look at the fruit and gifts of the Spirit in individual and congregational life.

CHAPTER 5

The Fruit and Gifts of the Spirit

A young woman who was searching for meaning in life was invited to join a small group. In high school she had made a commitment to Christ, but had chosen since to explore other lifestyles. In her third or fourth meeting, she reported to the group she was going to see her parents over the weekend. Before she could finish she began to cry. After regaining her composure, she informed the group that her parents were alcoholics. She did not know whether she could have a meaningful conversation with them. The group accepted her and supported her in the experience.

Some weeks later she renewed her commitment to Christ and covenanted with the congregation. As do all who covenant in that congregation, she gave her statement of faith in Christ and her reason for covenanting. She said, "I see how you love one another and I have experienced it."

We will now look at love, the fruit of the Spirit, at work in our lives and in the congregation. We will then seek to understand spiritual gifts: what they are, their relation to "natural talents," the need for training, and their crucial place in congregational life.

The Spirit Gives Love

The most basic sign of the Holy Spirit at work in an individual's life and in a congregation is the presence of self-giving love.

Jesus said, "By this all [people] will know that you are my disciples, if you love one another" (John 13:35, NIV). This kind of loving, according to Jesus, takes a source beyond ourselves. It needs a "miracle" explanation.

In his high-priestly prayer, Jesus prayed, "I do not pray for these only, but also for those who believe in me through their word, that they may all be one; even as thou, Father, art in me, and I in thee, that they also may be in us, so that the world may believe that thou hast sent me" (John 17:20–21). Self-giving love grows out of a living relationship with Christ. Such love is explainable only by God intervening in our human condition through the incarnation. Through the finished work of Jesus—his life, death, resurrection, and ascension—God has come to remedy the weakness of our spirit through the indwelling Holy Spirit, the Spirit of Christ.

This brings into our lives self-giving love, the central characteristic of God. Paul writes to the believers in Rome, "God has poured out his love into our hearts by the Holy Spirit, whom he has given us" (Rom. 5:5, NIV). The word for "poured out" is the same word Peter used in describing the coming of the Holy Spirit on Pentecost (Acts 2:17).

Through receiving the Holy Spirit, God's extravagant self-giving love has been poured into our lives. In writing to the Galatians Paul calls love "the fruit of the Spirit" (Gal. 5:22–23). Love is the expression of the Holy Spirit within. We do not manufacture love; it is a fruit—the fruit of the indwelling Spirit with whom we walk in a growing faith relationship.

The Fruit of Love in Our Lives

The expressions of the Holy Spirit producing love in our lives are many. Let me think with you about four.

The personality of Jesus. The qualities that Jesus expressed in relating to people are to be seen in us. The fruit of the Spirit is a whole, singular. Yet it is many orbed and has many surfaces like a diamond. The fruit of the Spirit as love is expressed in joy, peace, patience, kindness, goodness, faithfulness, gentleness, and self-control. Embodying this fruit of the Spirit is part of attaining the full stature of Jesus (Eph. 4:13).

The prideful selfish self does not express these qualities. How easy it is to become impatient, to act unkindly, and even to lose self-control! Joy and peace are gone and we come to realize we are not expressing love. As we return to submit to Jesus as Lord, the one shaping our lives, and walk in a dependence upon the presence and power of the Spirit, we can grow in the fruit of the Spirit. In situations that test us we discover the extent to which the characteristics of Jesus have grown in our lives. In fact, it is in these difficult interactions that our reliance on the Spirit can grow and the fruit of the Spirit can increasingly be seen in us.

Love and violence. Since we receive the love of God when the Holy Spirit comes into our lives, what does that mean when we feel anger or distance or call certain people our enemies? Let us see what God's love is like and how it worked out in Jesus.

What kind of love has God poured into our lives (Rom. 5:5)? In verse 6 Paul writes that God loved us while we were powerless; Christ died for the ungodly. In verse 8 Paul states that God showed love to us in that while we were still sinners, Christ died for us.

Amazingly, while we were God's enemies, we were reconciled to God through the death of God's Son (Rom.

5:10). Even more, Paul tells the Corinthian believers that God in Christ was reconciling enemies to God and has "entrusted to us the news that they are reconciled" (2 Cor. 5:17–21, The Jerusalem Bible).

Enemies need an opportunity to accept God's news of reconciliation. If Christians fight to destroy the enemy, their opportunity to accept the good news is gone. God chose not to destroy the enemy but to suffer violence to the death.

Peter writes that Christians are to follow the same pattern that Christ followed. "Christ suffered for you, leaving you an example, that you should follow in his steps.... When they hurled their insults at him, he did not retaliate; when he suffered, he made no threats. Instead, he entrusted himself to him who judges justly" (1 Pet. 2:21–23, NIV).

This represented a change of mind for Peter. On the way to Jerusalem before the crucifixion, Peter told Jesus that suffering and death at the hands of the elders would never happen to Jesus. Jesus called him "Satan" and said that Peter looked at things from a human point of view, not from God's. Showing suffering love to the enemy is now the call, writes Peter, having experienced God's "enemy-forgiving love." To receive the baptism with the Spirit is to be filled with God's suffering love for the enemy, even to giving one's life instead of taking the life of the enemy.

Costly? God has done it first and knows all about its cost. Jesus did not engage in violence that injured or killed people. But he did experience and express feelings of anger (e.g., Mark 3:1–6; Matt. 23). Paul writes, "In your anger do not sin" (Eph. 4:26, NIV). As Christians we need to acknowledge our anger and learn how to express it in ways that do not injure others, rather than denying it and keeping it inside or becoming violent. Our congregational leaders need to model and lead us in how to deal constructively with anger in personal and congregational life.

Love and social justice. The fruit of the Spirit was expressed in Jesus as he served the needs of the poor, the lame, the sick, the demonized, the blind, and the oppressed. The prophet Isaiah foresaw the Messiah as one upon whom God had placed the Spirit. As a result, the Messiah would be concerned for justice. He would be sensitive to the cries and needs and hopes of all (Isa. 42:1–4; 61:1–3).

The text in Isaiah 61:1–3 is the one Jesus used for his sermon at Nazareth as he began his ministry. It is clear that the love of God in Jesus expressed itself not only in seeking to save the lost sheep of the house of Israel, but also in feeding the poor, healing the sick, and protesting the oppression of the people by the Jewish leaders.

To be baptized with the Spirit is to receive the love of God in our lives. If the expression of our experience with the Spirit remains on the emotional high and on celebrative worship, we are not fully expressing the Spirit Jesus received in his life. As individuals and congregations, our profession that we have the Spirit within us will be tested by how much we join Jesus and the Old Testament prophets with concern and ministry to the poor, the oppressed, and the downtrodden.

Love, the context and goal of spiritual gifts. What is the relation of the fruit of the Spirit (love) and the gifts of the Spirit (the ways love serves)? Though love is spiritual, it is not one of the gifts of the Spirit. Love is the fruit of the Spirit in our lives, expressed in our character and in our relating to others.

Spiritual gifts are abilities to serve God and others (a fuller definition comes later). To the Corinthians Paul writes that spiritual gifts used without love are worthless to the user (1 Cor. 13:1–3). He then describes the qualities that love expresses and calls the readers who exalted certain spiritual gifts to make love their aim while desiring all the spiritual gifts (1 Cor. 13:4—14:1). This Paul calls the "more excellent way" (1 Cor. 12:31).

Furthermore, in Ephesians 4:1–16 Paul begins with the focus on the quality of loving relationships as the way to fulfill our calling. Paul goes on to say that Christ gives a spiritual gift to each one so the fullness of the ascended King may fill everything. It is through congregations releasing spiritual gifts in the context of love that Christ is seen as a loving presence in surrounding communities.

Paul further states in Ephesians 4:15–16 that in the context of speaking the truth in love, "the whole body ... grows and builds itself up in love, as each part does its work" (NIV). The purpose of spiritual gifts is to build the body in love. Love is the context and the goal in the use of spiritual gifts.

Jesus did not say, "People will know you are my disciple when you exhibit great spiritual gifts." Instead he said, "By this all [people] will know that you are my disciples, if you love one another" (John 13:35, NIV).

Even more strongly, Jesus in his prayer in the garden indicated that when all the disciples are one, living in union with God and Jesus, then the world will believe in the incarnation (John 17:20–21). This becomes the setting for evangelism.

The call to the primacy of love above spiritual gifts should guide our relationships when we discover differing views about certain spiritual gifts and their use. It should also guide us in the purpose toward which we exercise spiritual gifts.

Congregational Relationships and Evangelism

What does the fruit of the Spirit have to do with evangelism? In the letter to the Ephesians Paul presents a vision of what God is up to in the world and of our part in that vision.

Paul writes that it is God's "plan for the fulness of time, to unite all things in him [Christ], things in heaven and things on earth" (Eph. 1:10). We are made alive through God's rich mercy as we come to Christ in faith. We are then brought into a new community in which all barriers are broken, a community in which the Holy Spirit dwells (Eph. 2). This community is a prototype, a first example, of the unity God wants to effect in Christ.

Then Paul writes, "I urge you to live a life worthy of the calling you have received" (Eph.4:1, NIV). The calling is to exhibit what God's purpose is as demonstrated in their congregation being united in Christ. Paul's admonitions point the same direction: Be completely humble and gentle. Be patient, bearing with one another in love, making every effort to keep the unity of the Spirit. Even the basic elements in your faith point to that kind of oneness, says Paul (Eph. 4:2–6).

Paul is writing that the primary way in which evangelism happens through the congregation is by the quality of loving and forgiving relationships in congregational life. Deeper experiences in the Spirit must result in being able to love and forgive each other. The absence of love, forgiveness, and acceptance raises the question whether the Spirit is present and being honored. It will make evangelism nearly impossible. People may be brought to Christ and to the congregation, but after a year they will probably no longer be attending.

How instructive this is in our attitudes toward one another about our relationships and the use of spiritual gifts. Paul writes that love does not insist on its own way (1 Cor. 13:5). I am not to insist everyone should have the same spiritual gift I have. I am not to insist others cannot have a certain gift because I do not have it or that they cannot use it in our congregation. I am not to insist on using my gift in a way that destroys loving relationships. The use of spiritual gifts in loving relationships demands that we submit the prideful self to the Lord and to one another. Spiritual gifts will be used in ways that express God's broken heart in wanting everyone to be saved.

The indwelling Spirit is to flow out of us as living water to help others find Christ to quench their thirst. As William Temple wrote, "No one can possess (or rather be indwelt by) the Spirit of God and keep that Spirit to himself. Where the Spirit is, he flows forth; if there is no flowing forth, he is not there." Another writer says, "We must beware of any claim to the fullness of the Spirit which does not lead to an evangelistic concern and outreach." These are searching words.

The Holy Spirit is given that we may be witnesses of Christ, witnessing boldly with power. Peter and John said, "We cannot help speaking about what we have seen and heard" (Acts 4:20, NIV). Jesus had promised the disciples that the Holy Spirit would give them what to say when they would appear before the authorities (Mark 13:9–11). In the book of Acts the Spirit clearly empowers believers in the midst of persecution. The Spirit is the moving force in evangelism.

The Spirit Gives Spiritual Gifts

Looking at love as the context for the operation of spiritual gifts has led us now to look more fully at the nature of spiritual gifts and their function in the individual and the congregation.

Paul, in writing to the Corinthian church, says there are different spiritual gifts (1 Cor. 12:4). The word in the original language is "charismata." From this word the "charismatic movement" got its nickname, since one of its concerns was that the full functioning of all the spiritual gifts present in the New Testament take place in congregations today.

One way of understanding the relation of the Holy Spirit and spiritual gifts is that the *gift* of the Spirit gives union with Christ and empowers for service, while the *gifts* of the Spirit are used to do service.

Two items help set the framework to understand spiritual gifts. Paul writes that to each Christian a spiritual gift is given (Rom. 12:6; 1 Cor. 12:7; Eph. 4:7). Gifts are not given to special people only.

Every believer receives one or more spiritual gifts. Our congregations should help us to discover and release those gifts.

The second important item is that spiritual gifts are to build the body in its life and mission (1 Cor. 12:7; Eph. 4:12–16). Gifts are received individually but they are not private. In a sense they belong to the body: to discover, to train, to release, to affirm, and to support. This should help us avoid ego trips about our gifts.

What is a spiritual gift? A spiritual gift is:

- a service ability
- given by the Spirit
- in creation or redemption
- to one or more members
- to be used under the guidance and power of the Spirit
- in the context of the body
- to build the body in its life and mission.

The passages in the New Testament which list spiritual gifts are Rom. 12:6–8; 1 Cor. 12:8-10, 28; Eph. 4:11; and 1 Pet. 4:9–11. The abilities listed are used either in worship of God or in serving other persons, whether within or outside the body. Spiritual gifts enable the congregation to fulfill its ministries to God and to people.

From where do these spiritual gifts come? Paul tells the

Corinthians (12:11) that spiritual gifts are "all [the] work of one and the same Spirit, and he gives them to each one, just as he determines" (NIV). The gifts in Ephesians 4:11 are given by the ascended Christ. Since the Spirit operates for the ascended Christ, since some of the same gifts are mentioned in both 1 Corinthians 12 and Ephesians 4, and since Paul moves freely between Christ and the Holy Spirit (see 2 Cor. 3:17–18; Rom. 8:9–11), we can say that the Spirit of Christ gives all spiritual gifts.

Paul writes that the Spirit keeps on giving gifts (present tense) as the Spirit chooses. How freeing this is! There is no place, then, for me to be jealous of your gifts nor you of mine. Neither of us can belittle the gift of the other. Neither can say that my gift is better than yours, or that I don't need the ministry of your gift (1 Cor. 12:14–26).

In fact, Paul does not appear to rank the gifts, except for prophecy. Paul encourages us to desire all the gifts, especially prophecy (1 Cor. 14:1). His statement in 1 Corinthians 12:31 is better translated, "But you are eagerly desiring the greater gifts" (NIV footnote). In contrast to this self-serving attitude, Paul writes, "I will show you a still more excellent way." He then describes love.

In an encounter with a person in need, the Spirit may give the gift of wisdom or the gift of knowledge. In another setting the Spirit may give the gift of mercy or of service. We should thus know all spiritual gifts and be expectant in faith for the Spirit to give them. This also means that while we may have one or more gifts the Spirit uses regularly, there may be other gifts for which this is not the case.

In another setting or another congregation, other gifts may emerge and flower. Let us not put ourselves or other people in boxes. The Spirit delights in seeing spiritual gifts released. Let us become informed on spiritual gifts so our fears about them and their use can be removed. God gives gifts and they are good!

Is there any one spiritual gift which all believers are to receive? The classical Pentecostals and some charismatics say, "Yes," the gift of speaking in tongues. We saw earlier that in the stories of persons receiving the Holy Spirit in Acts, three of them mention speaking in tongues and three do not, though some evidence was present.

Many charismatics do not speak in tongues. Some charismatics say that tongues as a prayer language is available to everyone, but it is not *the* evidence of the baptism with the Spirit. Further, these people say that one should teach believers to claim this privilege.

Other charismatics are ready to leave the giving of gifts to people to the decision of the Spirit (1 Cor. 12:11). As Paul emphasizes the diversity in the giving of gifts (1 Cor. 12:29), he includes a three-letter word in his questions which implies a negative answer.

"Not all are apostles, are they? Not all are prophets, are they? . . . Not all speak in tongues, do they?" The implied answer is, "Of course not!"

Are there two kinds of tongues, a prayer language and a gift of tongues for speaking in public? Paul affirms the person speaking in tongues edifies himself (1 Cor. 14:4). When there is also interpretation of tongues, the church is edified, or nurtured, (1 Cor. 14:5). Since he speaks of these in the same context, are they not one gift used in two different settings?

Paul points the same direction in 1 Corinthians 14:28. He writes that if no interpreter is present, the tongues speaker should keep quiet in the church and speak to himself and to God. The same person uses the same gift in two different settings.

We note also that Paul is attempting to help the Corinthians bring tongues-speaking and prophecy under control in their worship services. How can a writer counsel against the overuse of certain gifts without the readers hearing the writer say he is against the activity? In 1 Corinthians 14:5 when Paul writes, "I would like every one of you to speak in tongues," he is not saying that they all should. It is not an imperative to be generalized to all believers.

Paul uses the same expression in 1 Corinthians 7:7 when he writes, "I wish that all [persons] were as I am," referring to his situation of being single. We cannot generalize Paul's first statement to mean that every believer is to speak in tongues without generalizing his second statement: every believer should be single.

Talents and spiritual gifts. The Holy Spirit is the creative expression of God at work. This was true in creation (Gen. 1:2) and continues to be true. All the abilities or talents we have are God's creative work in us. God is the source. The spiritual gifts given in 1 Corinthians 12:8-10, sometimes called miracle gifts, are also the creative work of God through the Spirit.

We can choose to view our abilities as the result of our cultivation and use them to achieve our self-centered goals, choosing to ignore God or to believe there is no God. Some Christians may also call these abilities "natural talents" and thus lose awareness of their source in God.

Some tension exists in the minds of some over the relation of "natural talents" and "spiritual gifts." As the result of the impact of science and technology, some persons view the work of the church as being done by our "natural" abilities. No other spiritual gifts are needed.

Another group of persons believes that only the "miracle" gifts given in 1 Corinthians 12:8–10 are spiritual gifts. Abilities which come from heredity and training are not spiritual gifts. They are only "natural" gifts.

The first group feels put down as second-class members because they do not have spiritual gifts according to the views of the second group. Thus they resist the idea of any "miracle" gifts being needed or even possible today.

The second group is concerned that the church allow all the gifts operating in the New Testament to be expressed today. These people are zealous to affirm the miracle-working power of the Spirit. They think that if "natural" gifts are acknowledged as spiritual gifts then the miracle gifts will be neglected. Each group has pushed the other more firmly into its position. Each is unable to hear the other.

The Scriptures can help these groups accept each other. The Hebrew mind did not know "natural" and "supernatural." All of life had God as its source and God moved through all of life. To speak of some abilities as natural talents and others as supernatural would have perplexed the early Christians. Teaching and administration were as much spiritual gifts as the gift of knowledge and the gift of healing (1 Cor. 12:8–10, 28).

Our abilities rooted in creation become spiritual gifts as much as those which are "miracle" gifts when we:

1. Confess their source is God (1 Cor. 3:21–23).
2. Use them to honor Christ as Lord (1 Cor. 12:3, 5).
3. Use them to build the body (1 Cor. 12:7).
4. Use them under the enabling power of the Spirit (1 Cor. 2:3–5; 12:6; 2 Cor. 4:7).

So we can say that spiritual gifts are the enabling empowerment by the Spirit. Sometimes the Spirit uses abilities from the created order and sometimes the Spirit provides what was not present in the person before.

If the Spirit operates sovereignly to build the church, the Spirit may choose to break in with miracle gifts. This is happening in many places today. Nowhere in the New Testament are we told God has withdrawn certain gifts from the church or that they are not needed. Rather we see an invitation to come with yieldedness to the Spirit and with readiness to receive the gifts the Spirit desires to give.

Paul views the full Godhead working through us in the release of spiritual gifts (1 Cor. 12:4–6). Paul is saying that while there are different gifts, there is one source—the Holy Spirit, not the Corinthians. While the Corinthians are to use these gifts in various kinds of service, they are to use them in devotion to the same Lord, not to exalt themselves. While there are different workings, they are all empowered by the same God at work in everyone. They are not empowered by the Corinthians' own abilities or ingenuity. What mind-blowing understandings! In spiritual gifts the Trinity is lovingly working through us, trusting us, honoring us. Praise be to God!

Some see 1 Corinthians 12:4 referring to charismatic gifts (vv. 8–10), verse five referring to service gifts (cf. Rom. 12:6–8), and verse six to administrative gifts (cf. Eph. 4:11). I doubt this, however. Paul uses *charismata* to introduce the list in Romans 12 as well as the one in 1 Corinthians 12. Are they not all "charismatic" gifts? In 1 Corinthians 12 prophecy is a charismatic gift. But are we to treat it as a service gift in Romans 12?

Paul uses the word *workings* in 1 Corinthians 12:6 as well as in verse 10 in relation to miracles. The focus is on the Trinity at work through all the gifts, thus countering the Corinthian tendency to exalt some gifts above others and to exalt themselves in the use of gifts.

No doubt there were other skills present in Paul's day which he did not include in the lists of spiritual gifts. These could include writing, tentmaking, carpentry, fishing, sailing, etc. Today many skills serve humankind while others serve in various settings in church life. These include typing, printing, computer skills, art, music, drama, and on and on. Are these skills spiritual gifts? They can be developed by Christians and non-Christians alike.

Let me illustrate the issue and at the same time point a direction for testing. In 1 Peter 4:9–11, Peter seems to be saying that hospitality is a spiritual gift. Hospitality includes the skills of cleaning, cooking, and arranging. But if only these skills are present, the gift of hospitality may be very lacking. There is a warm, gracious, and generous spirit involved in hospitality beyond the skills.

Skills are useful in carrying out the spiritual gifts of teaching, administration, serving, showing mercy, and the like. In themselves, skills are not spiritual gifts. When skills are used in a serving setting with a spirit of love and dependence upon the Spirit, the larger function of a spiritual gift can be served. Thus many skills are not spiritual gifts but are useful in the functioning of some spiritual gifts.

Training needed to use gifts. Just because one has received a spiritual gift does not mean that one knows how to use it so it builds the body. Let us look at this several ways.

Paul writes to the Corinthians that they were not lacking in any spiritual gift (1 Cor. 1:7). They were enriched in Christ with all speech and knowledge. Yet in 1 Corinthians 3:1–3 Paul calls them babes in Christ, not spiritually mature.

Thus it is clear that the presence of one or more spiritual gifts is not a sign that one is spiritually mature. One may be quite immature and do some unwise things with one's spiritual gifts.

This leads to a second consideration. Each of us needs help to understand our spiritual gifts—the purpose and contribution of each, and how to use them wisely. We see this in Paul's need to write to the Corinthians about their use of spiritual gifts (1 Cor. 12–14). They needed help in understanding the purpose of spiritual gifts and the interdependent relationship of spiritual gifts. They needed help to see that the quality of relationships between believers is the context for the use of gifts. The motivation of love in using gifts is more important than the gifts themselves. The Corinthians needed help to understand the use of several specific gifts: speaking in tongues and prophecy. Our need for these teachings is likely no less than the Corinthians'.

Paul writes about a similar concern to the believers in Ephesus (Eph. 4:1–16). Paul states our calling as Christians is to exhibit God's desire to heal all brokenness by loving, forgiving relationships in congregations. Each believer receives a gift to help the congregation in that work. Paul then notes that the task of church leaders is not to do the work of the church for members. Rather it is to equip the members for their ministry to build up the body in such loving relationships. Paul names a diversity of gifts in the leadership group (Eph. 4:11). In Acts and the epistles we learn this leadership was plural, sometimes noted with the umbrella word "elders" (1 Tim. 5:17; 1 Pet. 5:1). This leadership provides a firm basis for the training and release of spiritual gifts.

Thus all Christians need the training and wisdom of experienced leaders for the effective release of their spiritual gifts. Gifts are not used in isolation but in the context of the body, both when believers are gathered and when they are scattered in ministry. Such understandings rule out the use of any spiritual gift as a personal ego trip.

Spiritual Gifts and the Priesthood of All Believers

Paul's view of believers receiving spiritual gifts and ministering to others is one expression of the priesthood of all believers in the New Testament.

The work of the priest was to speak to God on behalf of the people and to speak to the people on behalf of God (see the story of Zechariah; Luke 1:5–22). God had wanted

Israel to be such a kingdom of priests but they did not catch the vision (Exod. 19:6). In the New Testament all believers are priests, called to declare the mercy of God to those around them (1 Pet. 2:9–10).

Thus spiritual gifts are involved in evangelism. The use of spiritual gifts in the life of Jesus is clear. Many times he used the gift of healing to heal physical illnesses and to exorcize demons. Jesus used the gift of knowledge in inviting the Samaritan woman to find living water (John 4:7–30). He knew information about her beyond what one normally knows about strangers.

As priests who are to serve God (Rev. 1:6), we have received the ministry of Jesus. Jesus gave his disciples the authority to do the ministry he did (Luke 9:1–2). The apostles clearly carried on the ministry of Jesus as reflected in the book of Acts. The "acts" of the apostles were the continued ministry of Jesus under the Holy Spirit.

Are we open to do the ministry of Jesus? Do we expect to see the gifts he used to be present in our ministries today? Do we experience the power of the Spirit which makes these ministries possible? Are we more children of our age than we are children of God's kingdom?

In the next chapter we will look at the context out of which the Holy Spirit renewal movement has come. Are there some conditions from the human side which help us understand why the Holy Spirit is moving among us in such a significant way? Are there lessons for us to learn? We will pursue this in the final chapter.

CHAPTER 6

Understanding the Holy Spirit Renewal Movement

In Galatians 4:4 Paul writes that "when the time had fully come, God sent his Son . . . " (NIV). In the coming of Jesus and the resulting spread of the church over the Near Eastern world, God moved in a fresh and mighty way. What happened has influenced history to our day.

Is there more than one fullness of time? The coming of Jesus and the establishing of the new covenant and its blessings are unique. On the human side of the fullness of time, there was a searching for something more, something beyond the unsatisfying religions of the day. The human spirit was open to the moving of God's Spirit.

Through history there have been times of openness to God's moving in special ways. We see this in the Reformation, the modern missionary movement, and major revival movements. Is there a "fullness of time" in our day in which we see God moving? I believe so.

At the beginning of this century, the Holy Spirit began to blow in a new way all over the world. In this chapter I will give a brief presentation of the historical context out of which the Holy Spirit renewal movement in North America has come. A brief overview of the renewal movement will follow, analyzing some of its contributions, some of its weaknesses, and some implications for congregations. The chapter will conclude with one approach to the basic elements in renewal.

Historical Context

From choice to no choice. We fail to realize that the early church grew rapidly when the choice to be Christian was set over against society and its various faiths. In that setting the Christian faith grew and prospered.

When Christianity became the state religion, police powers and the taxes of the state were used to support the Christian church. The whole society came to be seen as Christian. There was no choice involved. One became a citizen of the state by birth. After eight days one became a member of the church by infant baptism. Everything was done for the person by proxy; there was no choice. Church life became formal and ceremonial. It was no longer interested in meeting the needs of people.

Setting society free. The Renaissance focused on the human person and human abilities and the Reformation emphasized the importance of vocation and work. This set the stage for the Industrial Revolution of the eighteenth and nineteenth centuries. This was followed by the technological revolution of the twentieth century. People began to do things and invent things and control things that were never before imagined.

The setting free of society from the controls of the Christian church has been called secularization. Life is viewed as independent from God. One of the results of secularization is that identifying with the Christian faith demands a choice, a decision. One needs to make this decision in the context of many other options of faith, including secular humanism and a number of Eastern religions.

A second result of secularization in exalting the person

and human abilities was that the sense of the transcendent declined in most religious groups. God was worshiped, yes, but the human person was quite capable of handling life. The Lord Jesus was viewed as a good prophet, a great teacher, and the cross was simply a model of self-giving.

The need for God to deal with alienation, human weakness, and sin became refocused in following the prophet, his teachings, and the call to love like Jesus loved.

Wesleyan holiness. In reaction to the decline in emphasis on the supernatural, several other movements emerged. The background of one of these is found in John Wesley, a rector in the Church of England in the 1730s. Luther searched as to how he could be reconciled with an angry God; Wesley struggled with how he could find holiness in order to face a holy God.

We noted in an earlier chapter that Wesley developed a two-stage theology of Christian experience. The first stage is conversion, having one's guilt forgiven. Then one must search for Christian perfection. In this second stage, one deals with the "residue of sin." We call it the sin nature, the "old self" (Rom. 6:6).

This was Wesley's gospel which spread in England and resulted in the Methodist church. It did a great deal for England. It made the society face its industrial problems, such as the oppression of children and women in factories and the need to upgrade labor.

The two stages of Christian experience came to the U.S. in the Methodist preachers, the circuit riders. In the U.S. it developed into the holiness movement during the 1800s and the 1900s, causing considerable controversy.

Pentecostalism born. In the late 1800s some groups in the holiness movement began to add a third experience, the "baptism with fire." Out of this came another major movement. In 1906 on Azusa Street in Los Angeles, a revival broke out that lasted for three years. The new feature was that to know that one had received the baptism with the spirit, one needed to speak in tongues. Modern Pentecostalism was born. The marks of classical Pentecostalism are that the baptism with the Spirit follows conversion and that one knows one has received it when one speaks in tongues.

Pentecostalism has spread around the world. After 80 years there are now an estimated 50 to 100 million Pentecostals. No other Protestant group has grown as rapidly. Regardless of what persons may think of their theology, God has used Pentecostalism.

Modernism and Fundamentalism. During the 1800s the emphasis on human gifts and the scientific method gave rise to the movement called modernism. Modernists view the Scriptures as inspired writings like Shakespeare's writings or those of any other great writer. The human person can develop and society itself is perfectible. All that is needed is to control war and poverty and the millennium will come.

As a counter to that movement, another movement arose in the late 1800s and early 1900s called Fundamentalism. It is at the other end of the continuum from modernism. Fundamentalism emphasizes the divinely inspired Scriptures, the virgin birth of Jesus and his divinity, the vicarious atonement, the forgiveness of sins, and the second coming of Christ. These are essential truths. Fundamentalism has made an important contribution.

Fundamentalism focused on right beliefs; Pentecostalism recognized the body and healing and subjective experience. This does not mean the Pentecostals did not have a theology; their focus was on experience. The Fundamentalist focus was on the right faith. If one believed right, one was saved.

Rational society. During the twentieth century our society has emphasized the intellect, the rational. Worship in

Protestant and Mennonite churches has become more and more oriented toward verbal expression and the realm of ideas. There is little room for the emotions, the body, and the intuitive.

In the United States (and elsewhere) churches have often identified with the state even though there was no state church. Many denominations supported the state in its policies. For example, most denominations supported the U.S. in World War I. There were few voices in the churches in the United States who opposed World War II. One of these was the outstanding Protestant preacher, George Butrick. In our own generation, the identification of conservative religion with our government's policies is obvious. We do not have a state church as there was centuries ago, but the separation of church and state is not all that clean today.

Search beyond the rational. As a result of the growth of technology, militarism, and the church as institution, some important things began to diminish. These include faith as experience, the recognition of emotions in worship, and the sense of community. So in the '50s and '60s and '70s a number of movements arose.

We knew the flower children as hippies because they had long hair, simple clothes, and were not always as clean as they might have been. Because of that and some loose sexuality, we often failed to hear what they were saying. They decried the emphasis on consumerism and technology. They said the world powers were dominating and destroying the little peoples of the earth. That is not life, they said. Life is where people love each other and are concerned about each other and care for each other. Can we hear what they were saying? We need not approve of their methods to admit that they were saying things the Christian faith has always said.

After this the "Jesus people" arose: converted young

people. Their leaders were not always wise, and some of them were false leaders. The Jesus people were outside the institutional church because the church did not have room for intentional community, for an emotional experience, and for a sense of covenant. The church was a Sunday morning gathering. It was intellectual, verbal, and not a community.

During the '50s and '60s astrology grew. The horoscope came into many newspapers. The rise of interest in Eastern religions accelerated. People were searching for something that science could not supply. Were we awake to what was happening?

In the early '60s, people wanted more than a rational head trip religion. Some began to find it in the charismatic movement which accepted both an understood faith as well as an experienced faith. It emphasized not humanism, but a supernatural God, a God present in the Holy Spirit. Many of these persons were church members and many had been saved, although some had not been saved.

The Charismatic Movement

The movement arose. Our Catholic friends say many Catholics were not saved. In the charismatic movement they became saved as well as baptized with the Spirit. Many Mennonites, Episcopalians, Lutherans, Baptists, Presbyterians, and others had been saved, but their lives were like a desert. The Bible was dry and prayer was not meaningful. Then they learned about the promised gift of the Holy Spirit, who could be experienced, who could be present in one's life. They reached out in faith and they experienced the Holy Spirit.

The recovery of a neglected area of faith and experience in the church will always bring with it some extremes. The Radical Reformation had many extremes. In fact, the Reformers and the Catholics wrote off the Anabaptist movement, largely because of the extremes. The central themes of Anabaptism (the believers church) are now the heart of church renewal around the world, within Catholicism and Protestantism and within independent church movements.

In the believers church, the church is community. Members do ministry and evangelism while the plural leadership trains the members. Members live out their faith in discipleship and use the methods of the gospel in solving conflicts.

Of course there will be extremes, but one need not repeat the Reformers' mistake by rejecting a movement because of its extremes. One might miss what God is doing in the new movement. If we want to be aware of the Spirit of God's moving around the world, we must look beyond the extremes.

Spread of the movement. In North America the Holy Spirit renewal movement has penetrated all the mainline denominations since 1960. It is estimated that more than 5 million Baptists are charismatic, about 2 million Catholics, 1.7 million Methodists, and 1.5 million Lutherans. On the basis of a recent survey, I estimate that between 10 and 15 percent of the members in the Mennonite Church are involved in the Holy Spirit renewal movement, including between 25 and 35 percent of the pastors. In one conference in the Mennonite Church about two-thirds of the congregations are involved in the renewal movement.

In Brazil and the Philippines there are more than a hundred thousand base churches. These are small gatherings of 30, 50, 70, or 80 Catholic believers led by trained lay leaders. They worship, study the Scriptures, and ask what the Scriptures have to say to their situation. Most worship in a charismatic mode, and they are alive. In some respects they are the twentieth-century Anabaptists.

When a Pentecostal revival came to the Methodist

Church in Chile in 1909, 37 Methodist Pentecostals were tried in a church court for being "irrational and anti-Methodist." The Pentecostals organized the Pentecostal Methodist Church later in the year. At the time, the Methodist Church numbered about 6,000. It now has about 5,000 members. The Pentecostal Methodist Church in Chile now numbers almost 2 million.

In Africa, independent Christian groups are arising. They are called independent because they have had no direct association with missionaries. Their perception of the gospel is not refined, but they are experiencing the gospel and are much aware of the movement of the Holy Spirit. Many are in the Pentecostal mode. In fact, by the turn of the century, there will likely be more Christians in the southern hemisphere than in the northern hemisphere. Most of them will be Pentecostal or charismatic.

Recently I talked with the overseas missions secretary of the General Conference Mennonite Church about their churches in the northern part of Latin America. I asked him about the character of those congregations. He replied that their style of congregational life is charismatic.

Charismatic theology. God is bringing in a fresh breath of the Spirit. The charismatic movement in North America is one expression. While some charismatics have borrowed Pentecostal theology, Catholics, Lutherans, Mennonites, and others have affirmed another theology. The latter see in salvation the new birth, the new mind. One experiences salvation when one turns away from the self-centered, proud, sufficient self to acknowledge that Jesus is Lord. In salvation God deals with the sin nature, with self-centeredness.

There is in salvation also the forgiveness of sins as persons experience Jesus as Savior. It is Jesus who reconciles us to God and gives us peace. Also in salvation is the promised gift of the baptism with the Spirit, through which we experience God's presence and power in our lives. All of this is to be part of our experience in conversion (or confirmation).

However, we should not assume that everyone who comes to Jesus Christ experiences everything our doctrine says. That is a misconception, particularly in a generation that has not emphasized the Spirit and has been open little to the miraculous work of God. We have used the Holy Spirit as part of our doctrine and ceremonies without inviting the Spirit into our lives and worship.

As a result we should not be surprised that we have members who are Christians who have not experienced the reality of the presence and the power of the Spirit in their lives. While it is God's intention that the baptism with the Spirit be a part of conversion, many church members today experience it as a second major experience. The baptism with the Spirit was available at the time of conversion, but they did not know about it or chose not to claim it. If one lays hold of the promise of the Spirit later, one does not have to build a two-stage theology to understand it.

We need a normative understanding of God's intention for our experiencing the baptism with the Spirit. However, our major focus should be that of Paul in Ephesians 5:18: "Keep on being filled with the Spirit." The question is, Do you know the reality of the Holy Spirit in your life as God's presence and God's power? Have you received the spiritual gifts God has intended for you? Have you as an individual experienced in your life what God has promised in the gift of the Holy Spirit?

That question is being answered affirmatively by many people around the world. Included are brothers and sisters in Africa and South America. Although the charismatic movement as such is no longer highly visible in North America, Martin Marty, Lutheran historian and professor at the University of Chicago, writes, "It is still a mighty powerful leaven." Whether it will remain that way depends on whether the church is open to what the Spirit will give.

Before evaluating the charismatic movement we should note what is called, "The Third Wave." The classical Pentecostal movement (1906) is the "first wave." The "second wave" is the charismatic movement which arose since 1960.

The "third wave" is a movement among many evangelical churches to take the ministry of Jesus in signs and wonders (especially healing) seriously as well as his teachings. There is a much stronger emphasis on the Holy Spirit and on more freedom in worship, but without the charismatic gifts of speaking in tongues and prophecy.

There is strong recognition of the conflict of the two kingdoms, a basic theme in believers church theology. One needs to distinguish this from the kingdom theology of the reconstruction movement.

This may well be another stirring of the Holy Spirit, similar to the charismatic movement. It is renewing congregations which are becoming active in evangelism. It is part of the larger renewing work of the Holy Spirit.

Some contributions of the movement. The renewing work of the Holy Spirit has made significant contributions to many individuals and congregations. For many the Holy Spirit has become a reality in their lives. They experience peace, joy, and the power of the Spirit in their daily walk. They receive spiritual gifts for caring ministry in new situations day by day. They gain a strong love for the Scriptures which come alive in daily study.

The Holy Spirit renewal movement has influenced many congregations. The songs which they sing give opportunity to express a broader range of emotions. Worship services often are somewhat more informal and may include a time when persons can share experiences and prayer concerns from the past week. Many congregations are giving more attention to discerning and releasing spiritual gifts in congregational life. There is more interest in evangelism and bringing other people into the fellowship, often through small groups which provide acceptance and support in growth in faith and witness. There is more readiness to become involved in the social implications of the gospel.

Some weaknesses in the movement. Since the Holy Spirit renewal movement is seeking to restore a neglected area of emphasis to the church, one can expect excesses and limitations as the movement finds its way. Often there is an emphasis on the emotional aspects of a crisis experience with the impression that this kind of experience is the only valid one. Among some groups there is the tendency to make the gifts of tongues, prophecy, and healing the major focus, and to minimize other gifts.

There is a tendency among some charismatics to "write off" the institutional church as not filled with the Spirit and hopelessly cold spiritually. There is often an unwillingness to be accountable and to enter into serious dialogue over issues of faith and church life. This last tendency especially affects those who allow their visions and inner sense of what the Spirit is saying to take authority over the written Word. Or it may arise from severe disappointment with the stubborn refusal of others to recognize the presence and work of the Spirit, or from seeing traditional Christians rejoicing at sports events while squelching all joyous celebrations in the church.

Some implications. Individuals who have experienced the renewing power of the Spirit have much for which to be grateful in worship. They want to share with others what they have found so meaningful and precious. Unless they exercise sensitivity and wisdom in this sharing, such persons soon become obnoxious to the very persons that they would like to help. Such persons would do well to follow the counsel of Jesus to persons whom he healed. He told them to go home and tell no one. To bubble over about one's experience before people ask questions is to give answers before they are ready to hear. When people notice changes in someone's life and want to know what happened, then they are more ready to hear.

Renewed persons with dramatic experiences must recognize that their experiences with the Spirit are not the only valid kind. Other experiences in which persons know the presence and power of the Spirit are equally valid. Congregations should thus develop an acceptance of a variety of spiritual experiences in the congregation, learning to affirm everyone's experiences as each one witnesses to the realities he or she has experienced.

Congregations can also seek a balance of emphasis on the rational with its focus on words and ideas and on the experiential with its focus on emotions and response. Such a balance is needed both in viewing Christian experience and in worship and fellowship.

Congregations can encourage more freedom in congregational worship. Encouragement and training can be given in the use of spiritual gifts in worship and in informal ministry to those inside and outside the congregation. Allow the Spirit to build a greater sense of community through common life groups for support and accountability.

Above all, develop the faith expectancy that God through the Spirit empowers and God will act in worship and in relationships of witness to glorify Christ. The renewal of the Spirit will lead to witness and evangelism.

Elements in Renewal

In conclusion, what are the attitudes and experiences

that help open us to the renewing work of God?

One day in studying Acts 2 it struck me that this account describes the renewal of religious people. The 3,000 were not pagans, they were religious believers. They were faithful. Many had traveled hundreds of miles to come to Pentecost. They were devout believers. What helped them open their lives to change? I believe there were four things.

First, Peter's sermon gave them a vision of God's gift and God's claim on them in a new way. Their eyes were opened to some provision, some promise, some call of God that they did not have and which God was calling them to accept. Whether renewal has to do with claiming the baptism with the Spirit or the renewal of spiritual disciplines, or stewardship, or holiness—all of these involve a sense of a new vision of what God is asking of us. That new vision breaks the old ruts and the old patterns.

Second, there was a new sense of personal need and brokenness in the face of God's call and a response to God's mercy. "Men and brethren, what shall we do?" A congregation, a denomination, or a country will not be renewed unless there is a deep hunger and a thirst beyond the status quo. If our affluence, consumerism, and ability to make congregational machinery run and look respectable on Sunday morning are all that we want—God forbid!—that is all we are going to get. But if we have an inner hunger, if we are aware of an inner desert dryness, and a thirsting for the artesian well of the Holy Spirit, then God can give it. God will respond. Jesus promises this in Luke 11:13 where he teaches that God will give the Holy Spirit to those who continue to ask (ongoing action).

This second element is a key condition in renewal. Jesus said, "If any one thirst, let him come to me and drink.... Out of his heart shall flow rivers of living water" (the Holy Spirit; John 7:37–39). The 120 waited in prayer for God's timetable in the coming of the Spirit. Cornelius prayed to God regularly. The earnest prayers of needy people are an essential part in God releasing renewal in us individually and in our congregations.

Third, there was a new motivation for worship, fellowship, and witnessing. God's gift is so much beyond our thinking. How great is God's mercy that God should change one's life and give one the gift of the Holy Spirit! My own self-sufficiency and self-love are proud and full of illusions. When I get in touch with them, I realize I put Jesus on the cross. In love God has forgiven me. Praise God for God's mercy! It brings a new motivation and a new joy in living and in worship.

Finally, there was a sense that God was acting and inviting them to invest in God's kingdom. There are new priorities which put the kingdom first.

These are four basic elements in any renewal. It is my conviction that renewal (re-creation) is the work of the Holy Spirit as much as in creation. The Spirit of Christ creates and re-creates the church. Aligning ourselves with these four elements readies us to be instruments of the Spirit in renewal. Our own renewal is a necessity before we can expect God to use us in the renewal of others.

Claiming the Promise

I would like to close on a more personal basis. What is the Spirit saying to you by way of this teaching? What is your awareness and experience with the Holy Spirit? If Paul were to ask you, "Did you receive the Holy Spirit when you believed? Do you know the Holy Spirit as God's presence and power in your life?"—what would your answer be? You may say, "No, I don't know the reality of the Holy Spirit in my life." You may say, "Yes, but I have let it grow dry." Or you may say, "Yes, and it's been deepening ever since. Praise the Lord!" I would like to invite you to make the decision the Holy Spirit is now asking you to make.

While serving as a college campus pastor, I led a chapel to interpret the charismatic movement to students and faculty. I arranged for two young men to come on to the platform in the chapel with the one saying to the other, "Here is a gift certificate from a store uptown for your birthday."

"How do I know it is any good?" the other responded.

"You take it to the store and they will honor it," the first replied.

"I think I'll check out the store's rating with Dunn and Bradstreet first. No thanks, I won't take it."

The first student laid the certificate on the pulpit and they both left the platform.

I then gave a brief meditation on 2 Corinthians 1:18–22, saying that Jesus is God's "yes" to every promise God has made. Further, God has placed God's seal of ownership upon us and has placed the Holy Spirit in our hearts as a deposit which guarantees what is to come. God has promised the gift of the Holy Spirit in our lives. No matter how many promises God has made, they are "yes" in Christ.

I then held up the gift certificate and said, "The first person who comes may have it." The listeners were very quiet. Faculty are not in the habit of giving away gift certificates. Finally a young woman came.

I asked her if I could ask her a few questions. She responded affirmatively.

I asked her why she came for it. "I needed it," she replied.

"Why did you believe the gift certificate was any good?" I asked.

She replied, "Because I knew you and trusted you."

I gave her the certificate. I doubt if she took it to her

room to put on a shelf to exhibit and say to her friends next Christmas, "Look at the beautiful certificate I got in chapel!" No, she took it uptown and cashed it in.

She expressed the need and the trust, and then acted so the promise became reality. Many Christians in congregations acted on the promise of the gift of the Holy Spirit in their conversion. Many others are acting on it in the Holy Spirit renewal movement.

The question is not, How many experiences have you had? The question is, Have you claimed the promise of God's gift so you know the presence and power of the Holy Spirit in your life for discipleship and ministry? I leave the question with you.

Scripture Index

Genesis
1:2 . . . . 23, 96

Exodus
19:6 100

Psalms
2:7 31
103:17 50

Isaiah
11:3 31
42:1-4 89
42:1 31
61:1-3 89

Ezekiel
11:5 23
33:25-26 46
36:25-28 46
36:25 49

Matthew
3:6 30
3:11 . . . . 30, 50
3:13-17 . . . . 30, 61
4:18-23 61
7:4 54
7:11 . . . . 12, 59
10:38 51
18:15-20 55
19:13-14 69
23 88
26:2-29 61

Mark
3:1-6 88
7:8 54
13:9-11 92

Luke
1:5-22 100
9:1-2 101
9:23 . . . . 48, 70
11:13 . . . . . . 23, 59, 115
14:25-35 55
15:11-32 49

John
1:32-34 32
3:1-16 48
3:5 . . . . 24, 56
3:22 31
3:34 32
4:1-2 31
4:7-30 101

7:37-39 . . 32, 38-39, 59, 116
7:39 32
12:27-33 32
13:35 . . . . .86, 90
14:12-17 75
14:17-20 24
16:7 32
17:20-21 . . . . . . .86, 90
20:21-23 32

Acts
1:4-5 . . . . 32, 56-57
1:5-8 75
1:5 . . . . . . 50, 52-53, 74
1:8 . . . . . .32, 41, 50, 53. 56-59, 61, 81
2 114
2:4 74
2:14-36 33
2:17 . . . . .45, 86
2:36-41 47
2:36-38 61
2:38-41 33
2:38-39 61
2:38 61
2:39 45
2:40-47 61
2:41-47 55
2:41-46 81
2:41 81
2:42-47 33
4:20 92
4:23-31 59
4:24-30 75
4:31 74
8:5-17 . . . . .34, 39
8:6 40
8:8 40
8:9-14 40
8:12 . . . . .39, 40
8:16 40
8:14-17 29
9:1-22 35
9:17-18 53
10 70
10:1-48 36
10:30-48 29
10:34-48 80
10:44-48 61
10:47 56
11:1-18 42
11:14-18 36
11:14-17 80
11:15-17 56
11:16 52
15 . . . . 26, 42
19:1-7 . . . . 37, 64
19:2, 5-6 60
22:6-16 35
22:16 . . . . 35, 53, 61

Romans
1:18-21 69
5:5-10 . . . . .81, 87-88
5:5 86-87
5:12-21 68
6:1-18 48
6:1-11 . . . . 53, 61
6:6 105
8:9-11 94
8:9 24
8:14 81
8:15-17 81
8:26-27 81
12 . . . . 55, 98
12:1-2 69
12:6-8 . . . . 93, 98
12:6 93
14:17 81

1 Corinthians
1:7 99

1:12-17 53
2:3-5 97
3:1-3 99
3:21-23 97
7:7 96
10:16-17 62
11:18-34 62
11:23-26 61
11:26 62
12—14 99
12 . . . . 55, 94, 98
12:3 . . . . 24, 43, 97
12:4-6 98
12:4 . . . . .92, 98
12:5 97
12:6 97-98
12:7 . . . . 81, 93, 97
12:8-10 . . . . 93, 96-98
12:10 98
12:11 . . . . .93, 95
12:12-31 52
12:12-27 61-62
12:12-13 53
12:13 . . . . .52, 62
12:14-26 94
12:25 55
12:26 55
12:28 . . . . .93, 97
12:29 95
12:31 . . . . .90, 94
13:1-13 43
13:1-3 89
13:4—14:1 90
13:5 91
14:1 94
14:4 95
14:5 95-96
14:28 95

2 Corinthians

1:18-22 117
1:20-22 50
3:17-18 . . . . 76, 94
3:17 23
4:7 97
5:14-17 48
5:17-21 88
5:18-21 49

Galatians

2:20 24
3:1-5 71
3:14 60
3:27-28 53
4:4 103
4:6 24
5:22-23 . . . . 81, 86
6:14 48

Ephesians

1:10 91
2 91
2:11-18 50
4 94
4:1-16 . . . . .90, 100
4:1 91
4:2-6 91
4:4-6 54
4:5 53
4:7-16 61
4:7 93
4:11 . . . . . 93-94, 98, 100
4:12-16 93
4:13 87
4:15-16 90
4:26 88
5:18-20 81
5:18 . . . . .76, 111

1 Timothy

5:17 100

Titus
3:5 . . . . 24, 56

Hebrews
6:2 53
9:10 54

1 Peter
2:9-10 101
2:21-23 88
4:9-11 . . . . 93, 99
5:1 100

Revelation
1:6 101

The Author

Student of the Bible, pastor, counselor, workshop leader, conference speaker—all these have prepared Harold Bauman to write this book.

Reared in Columbiana County, Ohio, he attended Goshen College and Goshen Biblical Seminary in Indiana. He did graduate work at Southern Baptist Theological Seminary, Louisville, Kentucky (Th.M., 1962), Union Theological Seminary and Teachers College, Columbia University, New York, New York (Ed.D., 1972).

After 11 years in the pastoral ministry in the Orrville (Ohio) Mennonite Church, Harold served as campus pastor at Goshen College for 16 years. As a staff member of the Mennonite Board of Congregational Ministries, he served as a teacher and consultant in the areas of leadership and worship for nearly 14 years, working with congregational leaders across North America.

Involved in the Holy Spirit renewal movement since the early 70s, Harold has spoken in conferences and led workshops for pastors and elders. He served for more than a dozen years as the liaison between Mennonite Renewal Services and the official bodies of the Mennonite Church. He has participated in the Charismatic Leaders Retreat at Glencoe, Missouri, and was a seminar leader in the North American Congress on the Holy Spirit and World Evangelization in New Orleans in July 1987.

An emerging congregation in Dublin, Ireland, called Harold and his wife, Elizabeth, to help in leadership training beginning in July 1988 for two years. They have four grown children and three grandchildren.